A Portrait of Stockbridge

~ From 500 BC to 2001 AD ~

by

Hugh Saxton

with contributions by
Hubert Earney
Monica Harding
Mick Lunn
Laurie Stares

and illustrations by
Kenneth Bramer
George Fulleylove
Anna Stone

Published by
George Mann Publications
Easton, Winchester,
Hampshire SO21 1ES
01962 779944

A CIP catalogue record for this book
is available from the British Library

ISBN 0-95-244246-9

George Mann Publications

CONTENTS

Figures

Cover photograph: A view of Stockbridge looking west from the hill south of Winton Hill (*courtesy of Dick Pugh*). See also figure 26. This photograph is available as a postcard in Broughton Crafts.

Foreword

'I have a deep feeling for Stockbridge, its surroundings and its people, indeed I am one of them myself. Stockbridge, in my time, was an exciting, lively place to live in; there was always something going on. The vague feeling of connection with the past horse racing and traditions of training, the strong and lively sporting life, the clubs, the pubs, the religious life, the public traditions, the societies, the fishing club, the shops, the 'characters', the wide busy street which invited friendly intercourse and the general air of bonhomie amongst the Stockbridge people made life feel very worthwhile. I always felt safe within its peaceful boundaries. It is difficult to describe the pleasant feeling of arriving, once the train came to a standstill at the station and one could hear George Dalton's voice crying out; or when one crossed the station bridge or the Test bridge into Stockbridge itself – we were home.'

Tony Parker, born in 1927, lived in Stockbridge till 1961

The universal appeal of Stockbridge surreptitiously invades the affection of all who visit. Hugh Saxton successfully encapsulates its spirit in this, his tribute to our unique village.

Christopher Robathan, Lord of the Manor

During the many village meetings to discuss how we should celebrate the Millennium we were delighted when Hugh Saxton suggested a book on Stockbridge, giving a picture of our community, its past and its present. We know that it has meant a large amount of time and effort but the outcome is interesting and informative and we are all grateful to him.

David Basely, Millennium Committee Chairman

Acknowledgements

This book began with support for the project by the Millennium Committee under David Baseley. Since then he, with Catherine Cathcart-Jones and George and Eve Fulleylove have formed an invaluable advisory committee.

The major contributions by the late Monica Harding, and by Hubert Earney, Mick Lunn and Laurie Stares are acknowledged on the title page. They bring the book to life again and again. Laurie has also been a continual source of information and of confirmation of facts. His contributions of particular points are indicated by the initials LS. Similarly the initials GM indicate that a piece of information was supplied by Geoff Merritt whose knowledge of Stockbridge history is also profound. He read the manuscript and supplied fresh information and correction in good measure. David Allen, Andover Museum and Iron Age Museum, kindly read the historical section and made helpful suggestions. However any errors in this section are my responsibility.

I owe a particular debt to Liz Lourie who has twice been through the manuscript and commented with a refreshing and enjoyably acerbic freedom. There is no doubt that it is a better book as a result. Chris Clark also read and commented on the text and contributed the section on the Stockbridge Amateur Dramatic Society. John Stephenson provided the section on the churches. George McMeekin wrote the account of the Town Hall and David Webster the details of the Scout Hut. From Derek Tempero I learned the main facts about the Canal and the Railway, the racecourse and many details of wartime events and changes.

The elegant maps by the late Kenneth Bramer have added enormously to the book. So too have the charming drawings by Anna Stone. George Fulleylove supplied some of the modern photographs while Mrs Marjorie Butler, Jill Harding, Edward Roberts, Ray Standfield, Laurie Stares and Derek Tempero have all kindly lent photographs of older times in Stockbridge. I am also indebted to Dick Pugh for the use of his photograph of the town which is on the cover and is printed from a postcard available in Broughton Crafts. Figure 3 is reproduced by courtesy of The Francis Frith Collection, Salisbury, Wiltshire, SP3 5QP.

Many others have given me details of their businesses and their names are set out in the list of shops and businesses. Mrs Eve Lane and Mrs

Marion Paviour have been particularly helpful in this area. Maurice Jones, David Owen and Malcolm Crabtree provided much of the detail about Longstock and this was aided by Sandy Burnfield. David Owen also read the sections on Longstock and the Test. Mrs Shirley Owen kindly lent the 1965 Longstock WI scrapbook.

Christopher Robathan, Lord of the Manor, gave permission for the use of an abridged version of his address to the Courts Baron and Leet in March 2000. He and the Courts Baron and Leet have also given generous help with the costs of production of this book. David Baseley and the Parish Council have also given their support.

In addition, a number of people have provided information or ideas or pictures which have found their way into the text. For reasons of space I have not always acknowledged these contributions but I am, nevertheless, grateful to all of them:

> *Sylvia Baker, Christina Bourne, Marjorie Butler, Tony Cathcart-Jones, Ena Croker, Simon Francis, Bernard van Galen, Sonia Gubb, Sandy Hammett, Ray Hill, Stan Holdaway, Philip Hooper, Michael Johnson, Mollie Knox, Eve Lane, Christine Leslie, Freda Marchant, Wendy Morrish, Gordon Pearson, Arnold and Joyce Pye-Smith, Guy Robinson, Roy Owen Reece, John Robinson, Paul Robinson, Len Smith, Derek Tempero, Anthony Traill, Mary Tuff, Elizabeth Viney, Dave Webb, Reg Willis.*

Throughout the preparation of this book my wife, Julia, has patiently put up with my preoccupation, helped to decide on phraseology and content, has proof-read with great care and has been a constant support.

Finally I would like to thank George Mann for his help and advice during the preparation of the manuscript for publication and Barbara Large for her editorial skills.

Hugh Saxton

1 Welcome to Stockbridge

...drivers may have to thread their way round stationary vehicles...or wait while a duck leads a troop of ducklings across the road. At other times juggernauts and massive tractors rumble through...

To see Stockbridge at its most quietly appealing, and to appreciate how it used to be, come early on a summer Sunday morning. The High Street, steeped in sunlight, is peaceful, with scarcely any traffic. Early risers stop at Groves' for a newspaper and then, as if drawn by the fragrant smell of baking, go round the corner to buy bread or croissants from Lillie. Now and again a dog is walked down to the Common Marsh. On some Sundays churchgoers are hurrying to eight o'clock communion. As you look along the wide street with its pleasingly varied houses and shops, you see the hills rise at each end, the green of trees, hedges and grass contrasting with fields of hay or sometimes of ripening wheat and barley. At such times Stockbridge, lying across the valley of the River Test, could be seen just as another quiet English market town, lucky to have escaped much of the change and development which has defaced so many other towns.

In fact, while Stockbridge is relatively unspoilt, it has not escaped change. True, there is very little intrusive new building and it is still a most attractive town, *(fig 1)*, which remains in the memory of many who pass through it. Yet it is not a sleepy place nor is it often so quiet. Come later or during a weekday and you find the High Street alive with traffic, some passing through, some stopping to call at one of the shops, galleries or places to eat. At the busiest times drivers may have to thread their way round stationary vehicles unloading or waiting to park. They will often slow for cars being reversed onto the roadway or wait while a duck leads a troop of ducklings across the road. At other times juggernauts and massive tractors rumble through, while overhead there may be the growl or whine and flutter of Army Air Corps helicopters from Middle Wallop. But it is the road traffic which makes Stockbridge what it is; a rural centre for shopping and other activities which outshines many towns ten or twenty times its size.

1 Stockbridge High Street, looking west from the roundabout which replaced the railway bridge in the early 1970s. This is the nearest view to compare with the one taken from the railway bridge in fig 14 but is from a lower point.

And it is a town which has run counter to the trend among rural communities to lose shops, pubs, schools and other facilities.

It is even a tourist attraction, especially at weekends. Visitors come simply to enjoy the town; to wander along the patch-worked pavements, to look in shop or gallery windows or to feed bread to the trout and ducks in the bend of the river opposite Stokes' Garage. They buy cards in Broughton Crafts, eat a baguette at Lillie and walk down to the Common Marsh to enjoy the open space, the bird life and the silver gleam of the lazily rippling river. If they look carefully they will see trout keeping station among the weeds or suddenly darting up or downstream. Stockbridge has given and continues to give pleasure to many people, whether they live here or simply visit us.

These are some of the reasons for writing a book about Stockbridge in this millennial year. It describes the origins of this unusual town, something of its history and the story of some of its inhabitants today, so different from its past. The aim is to give a picture which captures the life of the town now and in the past; a picture which those in the future can use to compare with the Stockbridge of their time. Few people think of themselves as part of history, but this book is written in the knowledge that the clothes, cars and customs of today will seem quaint or strange or charming to our descendants. However that may be, we in the Millennium year enjoy life in this town and hope you will enjoy reading about it.

A town or a village?

Is Stockbridge really a town? In terms of the population, with barely 500 people on the electoral register, probably not. It has very few streets and the High Street has even been jokingly compared to the film set for a Western, because there are so few houses behind it. It has a friendly village atmosphere and many of its inhabitants think of it as a village. On the other hand, it has nearly 50 enterprises: shops, galleries, pubs and places to eat; it has a doctor's surgery, a firm of solicitors and a number of businesses. There is a post office, a bank and a fire station. There are four churches. It has a Lord of the Manor. It also has a Town Hall. On balance, it seems fair to call it a town, if only as a courtesy title. That is what I have done in this book but either word is valid.

One reason for its small population is an anomaly of its western boundary. Although the houses on the west side of the Test have a Stockbridge address, they are actually in the civil parish of Longstock. Their council taxes go to its parish council and they vote in Longstock. In other words, they belong to both communities but are not counted as part of the population of Stockbridge. Because the ground in the valley floor is peat-soft, regulations now demand that new houses there must be built using pilings. Since this appreciably increases the building costs, it is on the firmer land each side of the valley that new houses are most likely to be based, perhaps adding further to the future population of Longstock.

2 The Origins of Stockbridge

From prehistory to the Norman Conquest

It is not easy to imagine the days when our area was peopled by prehistoric men and women but they have left much evidence that they were here, most of all in the massive earthworks of the Danebury Hill-fort *(fig 2)*. There are many arguments about the time when modern man first appeared, but for at least some ten thousand years there have been men and women with bodies and brains like ours, with the same needs for food and drink, shelter and warmth. We can feel sure that they loved and hated, laughed and felt fear as we do today. They did not have our technology but they had their own solutions to the problems of living. At first, they used stone and flint tools as had their forebears during the two million years of the Stone Age. Then, in about 2000 BC, someone discovered how to make bronze. It was the best available material for tools until, around 800 BC, the way to smelt iron was discovered, bringing in the Iron Age.

For much of prehistory man was a hunter-gatherer, expert in what today we would call survival skills, but there is evidence that there were farming communities in Wessex from the fourth millennium BC and this activity increased in the centuries which followed. The visible indications of prehistoric

2   Aerial view of Danebury Hill from the east. Trees have grown in the central area, once the site of the Iron Age communities. There are also trees on the ramparts, though many have been felled because of disease *(courtesy of David Allen)*

agriculture are relatively few but aerial photography has shown numerous field systems and farms dating from the second millennium BC and there are many barrows (burial mounds) also from these times.

Stockbridge lies between the sites of three enclosed settlements dating from the Iron Age in the first millennium BC. These are Danebury Ring, Meon Hill and Woolbury above Stockbridge Down. Danebury is the most striking and has been extensively investigated. The results can be found in a number of books and in the admirable Andover Museum and Iron Age Museum. They show that from about 550 BC till about 100 BC the site was occupied by communities who built a series of massive earth and wooden ramparts of some sophistication. This might suggest that they loved fighting but probably they were needed for defence and it is likely that the periods of peace were much longer than those of war.

The excavations revealed that the Iron Age community was technically quite advanced. They traded widely and this included links with the Continent. When not at war they lived in thatched homes within these forts and farmed all round the hill, using ox-drawn ards[1] to plough the land. Their nearest source of water was the Wallop Brook to the west and many of their pastures were close to rivers but it is not certain how water was brought to the hill fort itself.

Then, some time around 50 BC, something dramatic happened because the main gates of Danebury Ring were burned down. Was this part of a general change due to the growing Roman influence? We can only guess, but at about this time all the hill-forts in the area seem to have been abandoned, indicating a major change in the way of life. Whatever the cause, the Test Valley area was still being farmed and was occupied when the Romans came. There are indications of droveways from Danebury to the Stockbridge crossing. These possibly date from before and during the Roman occupation.

The Development of Stockbridge

What, then, is the connection between prehistoric man and Stockbridge? The answer is that from earliest times there was a need for places to cross the river. Even now the valley bottom is soft. Two thousand years ago it would have been very marshy. Stockbridge is located at one of the narrowest

[1] An ard was an iron tipped wooden implement resembling a plough, similar to many ploughs used today in India and Africa.

sites in the valley and on the eastern side the land slopes relatively gently. These factors make it an obvious site for a crossing. Men or animals moving across the marsh would want firm footing until they came to a fording place or log bridge over the river itself. At first this might have been achieved with bundles of faggots[2], plentifully available in prehistoric times. Later, chalk was imported in large amounts, from hillside quarries up and down the valley, to create a causeway across most of its width, leaving a ford or log bridge at the western end. The question then is, who started the causeway?

Some feel that the most likely builders of such a bridgehead were Roman soldiers, a professional force who included road and bridge-building among their skills. Professor Rosalind Hill pointed out that the early names of *Le Strete*, *Le Street* or *Lestrait* given to Stockbridge, are ones used for Roman roads. The only known Roman road from Winchester (Venta Belgarum) to Salisbury (Sarum) crossed the river at Horsebridge, below King's Somborne. However, when we talk of 'a Roman road', we mean one of a system of stone-surfaced roads linking main military centres, the equivalent of today's trunk roads. In some 400 years of Roman occupation, many lesser roads must have been built, but no artefacts have yet been found in Stockbridge to prove a Roman origin.

The straightness of the roads to Stockbridge from Sutton Scotney and on towards Salisbury also suggest a Roman construction. Another suggestive feature is the directness of the original road, Meon Hill, up the slope on the west side of the river. This is quite suitable for marching legions but is too steep a hill for any kind of horse-drawn vehicle. The more gradually sloping curved road now in use was built in the Middle Ages.

Despite these arguments there is no firm evidence as to who built the causeway. It could have begun with the Romans but the width of the chalk deposits is far greater than would be needed simply for a road. It is therefore possible either that it was all built in the Middle Ages or that more was added then to allow building of houses together with a wide street which gave space for a weekly market. If this is true it could explain the name *White Somborne* given to the settlement at this time[3].

[2] Bundles of faggots or withies were found when refurbishing the footings of the Grosvenor Hotel in 1938/9 and also when excavating to lay pipes for mains water supply and main drainage in the 1960s.
[3] Rosalind Hill believed that the name was due to the chalk face below the A3057 as it descends into Stockbridge from the south. Bob Edwards believes that there are difficulties with the suggestion that the whole causeway was built at one time and offers this as an alternative explanation.

Once established, the site of a good river crossing would attract traffic passing east-west, particularly from Winchester to Salisbury. It was inevitable that a settlement would grow up where a north-south route, linking Southampton with towns such as Andover and Newbury, crossed this road. However, there are no written records of Stockbridge in the centuries immediately following the Roman occupation, as successive waves of Angles, Saxons and Danes[4] first plundered, went home and later returned to settle in England. (*Wessex* is, of course, the territory occupied by the West Saxons.)

By the end of the first millennium, England was becoming united under Anglo-Saxon kings, notably Alfred, and the country was divided into shires. The latter were made up of 'hundreds', areas under a thegn, a noble of lower rank. Each hundred had its own court[5]. The hundred of King's Somborne included White Somborne or Le Strete, as Stockbridge was then known. The final series of Danish invasions early in the eleventh century led to the reign of Canute from 1016 to 1036 and, as with earlier invaders, the Danes soon became assimilated into English life. It is therefore no surprise that at the time of the Norman Conquest, White Somborne was held by a Dane named Tol under a grant from King Edward.

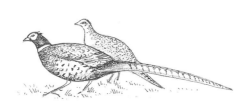

---

[4] The so-called 'Danish dock' in Longstock (Chapter 10) is a reminder of this period.
[5] The law officer, or 'reeve', of the shire was a 'shire-reeve' – hence 'sheriff'. There were also hundred-reeves.

2 The Norman Conquest to the Twentieth Century

After the Norman Conquest the principle that every area should be the responsibility of a lord became more firmly established, adapting the Anglo-Saxon system. All land was owned by the King. The barons, and below them, the knights, held land for which they paid a rent or tax to the King. The Domesday Book was a record of the resources on which these taxes could be based. The knights might also have to fight for the king if it was required. The knight who had the use of the land held it as a 'manor' with its own court of which he was lord. His 'demesne' was the manor-house and the adjacent lands which he kept for himself.

The lord had the right to a certain number of days of labour on his land[6] from his serfs or villeins. Even though bound to his service, they also had strips of land of their own to till and a share, or 'stint', in the use of the village pasture, the hay meadow and the village woodland, where the swine and geese were turned loose. Such lands shared in common were the forerunners of the commons still found today. Within this system there were also some freemen who held land with no obligation of service but instead they paid rent to the lord. Initially their numbers were small.

Boroughs and Burgesses

When Alfred was consolidating his resistance to the Danish invaders he had instituted a series of 'burhs' or fortified towns. Their relative safety led them to develop into centres for trading; hence the name 'borough' given to a town with a charter for trading and later to one with the right to send members to parliament. A fee, paid to the king, gave the right to hold markets and to trade. The burgesses, or freemen, could build houses on 'burgage plots' which gave the right to buy and sell in the markets. Later, boroughs sometimes developed at unfortified sites. Borough status made a town independent of the lord of the manor. No-one is sure when Stockbridge became a borough. What follows is a brief summary of the

---

[6] Part of his land would be among the strips held by his serfs. All were cultivated to a common pattern, e.g. wheat in year 1, fallow grazed by cattle in year 2 and oats in year 3. Of course cereals would be unlikely to be grown in the marshy valley bottom.

main points in the argument.

The Domesday Book, in 1086, shows that the manor of Somborne, within the hundred of King's Somborne, was held by William d'Eu or d'Ow. It is likely that this was Stockbridge. The manor had a total of 37 men bound to the lord. Nine houses belonging to burgesses were also listed, but it is possible, even likely, that these were not actually in Stockbridge itself, just as a landowner today may have outlying properties.

In 1096 William d'Eu was executed for treason and the manor reverted to the Crown. Nearly a century later, in 1190, it was granted to William de Briwere by Richard I. The first indication of borough-like status comes at this time when Richard I granted William the right to hold a weekly market in Lestrait. This was renewed by John in 1200 and in 1221 Henry III added the right to hold an annual fair, which continued till 1932. All such grants would have required payment to the king but they did imply recognition of the existence of a town. The market would, of course, have brought in money from the resulting trade. Later in the century, as the town expanded, new plots of a pattern similar to burgage plots[7] were recorded, reaching 97 in 1283 when our ancient courts began. By then the town was, in some respects, behaving like a borough and its citizens were sometimes referred to as burgesses.

After the death of William de Briwere a sequence of inheritances and marriages led, in 1399, to Somborne becoming a part of the estates of the Duchy of Lancaster, which returned the property to the Crown. No manor-house was ever built in or near Stockbridge, probably because William de Briwere and all subsequent heirs had extensive estates elsewhere. Ultimately the Duchy of Lancaster sold the manor to Joseph Foster Barham in 1824. No borough charter has been found. However, when Queen Elizabeth granted the right to send two members to Parliament in 1562/3, it may be taken as a de facto recognition of borough status. Most writers have described Stockbridge as 'a borough by prescription', meaning that its status is based on long-continued use.

---

[7] This cautious phrase is because a true burgage plot is one in an established borough. Many of the gardens of houses on the north side the High Street are strikingly long and narrow (see figure 35). This is similar to the pattern in burgage plots elsewhere and presumably reflects the need to give a frontage on the street to as many individuals as possible. The layout on the south side was similar but later developments here have removed the evidence.

A Moment from the First Civil War

Accounts of the history of Stockbridge reflect the relative obscurity of the town. However, during the civil war between King Stephen and Empress Matilda (the period of Ellis Peters' Cadfael books), Robert, Earl of Gloucester was captured at Stockbridge. He was protecting the escape of his sister, Empress Matilda, who was fleeing with her army from King Stephen's forces. He was later exchanged for Stephen, who was a prisoner.

A New Bridge: the Plague Strikes

Such records as there are show a pattern of expanding activity for some time. Early in the fifteenth century the main bridge over the Test was restored at the expense of three citizens of Winchester as an act of piety. The bridge was inscribed with the request for passers-by to say a 'pater noster' and an 'ave' for the souls of its founders and makers. Later in the fifteenth century the town for a time became almost deserted, probably because of the plague[8]. The market was temporarily discontinued, but by the time of Henry VII, in the late fifteenth century, life was returning to normal. In 1799 the bridge was widened and repaired at the expense of the County of Southampton *(fig 3)*. The substantial stone piers of this bridge were the cause of repeated floods. It was even said that the old bridge was so low that ducks had to lower their heads to pass under it! In 1963 it was replaced by the modern bridge *(fig 4)*.

A Rotten Borough

In 1562-3 Queen Elizabeth granted the town the right to send two members to Parliament. Although a fee was required to send a member, so that some boroughs did not take up the right, Stockbridge did send members, mostly drawn from the local gentry. The first two members were returned by only seven electors! In 1614 28 voters were recorded and in 1793 there were 63 voters. By then the habit of selling votes to the highest bidder was well established. Sometimes the bribe was in kind; for example, Essex Strode's gift of a silver mace in 1681 or the present of a lovely set of communion plate by George Pitt and Thomas Jervoise in 1697. Both these are still held by the town and church respectively. The most unusual bribe was the reported offer by Sir Richard Steele in 1713. He was said to have

---

[8] It is believed that there was a plague pit in the old St Peter's Churchyard at the southern corner away from the road. (GM)

3 The 'old' Test bridge viewed from the south. Its relatively thick pillars and narrow arches caused some obstruction to the river above this level and led to repeated floods in the town at times of increased flow. This bridge was demolished in 1963 *(courtesy The Francis Frith Collection)*

stuck a large apple full of guineas saying that it would be a prize, presumably if he was elected, for the man whose wife was the first to give birth nine months later!

Later it became more usual for the votes to be sold for money and this favoured men from outside the area with large fortunes. The system of extracting these 'fees' was well organised and in the time of John Bucket, landlord of the King's Head Inn, the sum of 70 guineas[9] was the figure reached for a payment to the voters in 1790. The defeated candidates, George Porter and Joseph Foster Barham protested. In 1793 a select committee of the House of Commons investigated the claims of bribery and threatened the 63 voters with disfranchisement for having accepted bribes. Porter and Barham were then returned as members.

Barham was determined to increase his influence in the town. He bought property in the High Street and in 1790, with George Porter, built the Town Hall at their expense. By 1820 he owned 80 houses in the town, many of which he had built. At that point, in a period of temporary shortage of money, he sold 72 to Lord Grosvenor[10] who won the seat in 1824. Barham

[9] About £3,700 at today's values! It is said that John Bucket sent the Bailiff, Christopher Bishop, to the Wheatsheaf Inn at Popham (15 miles) to negotiate. The first offer was turned down and Bishop took a fresh horse to Popham, returning with the improved offer. A few years later Bucket is listed in the Hampshire Directory as a 'Gent' – see Appendix.

4　The present wide-span bridge, seen from a similar point. Vegetation hides the full width of the bridge. Since it was built there have been no floods in the High Street *(see page 108)*

kept some land and when his fortunes revived he built further houses to form Blandford Row[11] and Trafalgar Street, now the lane between Trafalgar House and The Homestead. Needless to say they housed voters favourable to him. He also bought the Lordship of the Manor from the Duchy of Lancaster. The story of the courts run by the Lord of the Manor is described in Chapter 4.

Lord Grosvenor gave his name to the Grosvenor Hotel, which was built on the site of the earlier King's Head Inn. Over the pillars of its portico is the curved room which is such a feature of the High Street and which is the club room of the Houghton Fishing Club. Lord Grosvenor did not remain as member for long, since Barham's son won the seat in 1831. By this time the Reform Act of 1832 was imminent and Stockbridge was one of the boroughs to be disfranchised. No more rich pickings.

[10] The title 'Lord Grosvenor' is that of the heirs to the Dukes of Westminster and does not therefore carry with it a seat in the House of Lords. In the 18th and 19th centuries it was not uncommon for such peers to seek election to Parliament.
[11] The standard to which the houses were built was the lowest possible: they were overcrowded and insanitary. Even in the 1920s and 1930s the conditions in which some of their inhabitants lived gave Blandford Row the name of 'Bug Alley'.

5 A remarkable photograph of Old St Peter's Church before its demolition in 1870, seen from the south. The chancel, whose roof is on the right of the picture, is all that survives today. The window in the roof may be the priest's bedroom mentioned by Monica Harding. The building on the left of the picture is the *White Hart.*

Churches in Stockbridge

For most of its early history the town did not have a church of its own. St Peter's Chapel, at the east end of the town, was a dependant or subsidiary of St Peter and St Paul, the church in King's Somborne This reflected the earlier position of King's Somborne as the centre of the manor. In 1842 it became St Peter's Church *(fig 5)*, but by 1863 the church was felt to be 'very old, damp and encumbered with massive stone walls and pillars and unfit for public worship'. In 1870 it was largely demolished but the chancel survives as Old St Peter's and a communion service is held there once a month[12] .

Its graveyard contains the well-known tombstone of John Bucket, with an epitaph in verse, given in the Appendix. In an extension of the churchyard across the road to King's Somborne are the graves of Commonwealth and British airmen who died in the first World War, through accidents at a training airfield on Chattis Hill, just off the road to Salisbury.

In 1866 a new church, also dedicated to St Peter, was built in the centre of the town, next to the Grosvenor Hotel. It contains some windows and other elements from the old chapel. Its spire, added in 1887, is one of the most prominent features of the town when it is viewed at a distance. As

[12] Monica Harding believed that there was an upstairs bedroom in the old church so that a priest from King's Somborne could sleep overnight after evensong in wintertime. See figure 5.

6   Drover's House in the Houghton Road. The old Welsh writing, roughly translated, means 'Seasoned Hay, Rich Grass, Good Beer, Sound Sleep'.

part of the millennial celebrations floodlighting has been installed.

In 1904 a Baptist chapel was built between Sheriff's House and what is now Stokes' Garage. St Thomas More's Roman Catholic church lies behind Rosalind Hill House on the south side of the High Street. Before this, in the 1920s, it was the town's first cinema, showing silent films.

No More A-Droving

The average herd was about 200 and could stretch for between three and four miles.

Two hundred years ago Stockbridge was used to seeing large herds of cattle or sheep, bred on the Welsh hills, being driven through. Some were to be fattened on the pastures of Hampshire or Sussex. For others the ultimate destination was London, where, in the last quarter of the 18th century '100,000 head of cattle and 750,000 sheep found their way to Smithfield annually' though most of these went by other routes. In the early 1800s this had reached 210,000 cattle and 1,250,000 sheep[13]. Probably many of the herds coming through Stockbridge were destined for Portsmouth or Southampton to victual ships, rather than for London. Drove

[13] The earlier figures are from the book by Bonser and the later from the article by Webb – see 'Sources and Further Reading' at the end of this chapter.

roads, or 'drift ways', with wide verges on which the animals could graze, were the main routes in use. The drovers from Wales were licensed for a year and had to be married and over 30. The average herd was about 200 and could stretch for between three and four miles. There was a guide ahead to warn farmers and to look out for an overnight stop. Sidesmen on foot controlled the herd. The head drover often carried goods or letters for people on the route and might also escort Welsh girls looking for work in the cities.

Drover's House in Houghton Road is a reminder of this trade *(fig 6)*. Its walls carry in Old Welsh the message 'Seasoned Hay, Rich Grass, Good Ale, Sound Sleep', a welcome to Welshmen on the move with their flocks. This was only part of what the drover required; for example, smiths expert in shoeing oxen were also needed. Droving gradually declined in the second half of the nineteenth century, with the coming of the railways, and disappeared altogether when cattle lorries appeared in the 1920s. Today when the name 'Drove' is applied to a road it is often linked to its past use, though it may simply be a trendy term for a road on a new building estate.

Days at the Races

The first horse box was made in Nether Wallop, enabling Elis to reach Doncaster in good condition and win the 1836 St Leger.

The training of racehorses in this district dates back to the end of the eighteenth century. The founder of the family concerned was John Day of Houghton, a successful trainer. His son, John Barham Day, became an outstanding jockey and at one stage was jockey to King George IV. In 1832, with support from Lord George Bentinck, he transferred his training to Danebury next to the Stockbridge Racecourse. The gallops and stables were improved and many winners were trained. Day was probably the first full-time trainer and the first to apply professional methods. In 1840 his filly, Crucifix, won the 1,000 guineas, Oaks and St Leger. A more interesting winner was Elis at the St Leger in 1836. Lord George had the first horse box made in Nether Wallop and sent Elis and another colt to Doncaster in it, arriving just before the race. By then the odds were heavily against them as it was assumed that they would have come on foot: Lord George won a large sum of money.

John Barham Day was succeeded as a trainer by his son, John Day, who was even more successful. In 1867 he sent out 146 winners. His stable jockeys were first, George Fordham and then Tom Cannon, who married Day's daughter, Kate, in 1865. Cannon later took over the training stables from Day and ran the Danebury Down Racecourse. When it closed in 1898 he bought the Grosvenor Hotel which still contains many memorabilia of the racing era[14]. Tom Cannon's great-grandson is Lester Piggott, the premier jockey of the 1970s and 80s.

It is hard to be certain when racing began in this area. One writer has said that it started in 1753. What seems clear is that it increased in popularity after 1831 when the Bibury Club in Gloucestershire transferred its races to Danebury. The Bibury Club and Stockbridge Races were an annual meeting held in late June. In 1867 a fine grandstand was built, replacing earlier wooden stands. At some stage a starting gate invented by Thomas Marshall was installed. The course became a major centre for racing.

Stockbridge race meetings were popular and well attended. One prominent racegoer was Lord Palmerston, Prime Minister for periods in the 1850s and 60s, who lived at Broadlands in Romsey, more recently the home of Earl Mountbatten. The most illustrious visitor was the Prince of Wales, later Edward VII, who regularly stayed at Hermit Lodge in the Houghton Road during meetings. A footbridge over the river links the garden of this house with that of Grosvenor House, now the White House. This is where Lillie Langtry would stay during the period when she was Prince Edward's mistress. A woman of outstanding beauty but no means, she had come to London in 1876. In little over a year she had become a celebrity, invited by prominent hostesses because her presence attracted other guests. She had her portrait painted by Millais and other artists, her face was on picture postcards and she was recognised wherever she went. She was rapidly taken up by the Prince of Wales and they were seen everywhere together. Their relationship only lasted three years but her visits left a lasting impression on Stockbridge. Her later career as an actress was less notorious but enabled her to achieve independence and a comfortable fortune.

The days of the racecourse ended in 1898 when part of the land was inherited by a lady who disapproved of gambling. The meetings were transferred to Salisbury. This was a major blow to the local economy but

[14] Cannon Lodge, in the London Road, (earlier called Springfield) was his home for a time and once had cannons on the gateposts.

the training of racehorses continued until the Second World War. 'Atty' (Henry Seymour) Persse of Chattis Hill bred and trained 'the Tetrarch', foaled in 1911, who became one of the fastest two year olds ever known. His colouring, grey with white splodges gave him the names of the 'Spotted Wonder' and 'Soapsuds'. He was never beaten and Stockbridge residents did very well by backing him but shortly before the Derby his leg was injured and he never ran again. A painting of him may be found on the screen in front of the vestry of St Peter's Church. Persse's most famous jockey was Steve Donoghue who, for a time, lived in Stockbridge.

The stables gave employment to farriers, smiths, saddlers and stable-boys. Many Stockbridge residents remember seeing strings of horses on their way to or from the station. Monica Harding recalled that a train was often delayed in its departure because a horse was reluctant to be loaded, making pupils late for school in Andover.

Pubs, Inns, Hotels and Breweries

A hundred years ago there were 13 pubs or inns as well as a brewery. The decline began when the racing at Danebury stopped.

Today there are five pubs or inns in Stockbridge, if the Grosvenor Hotel is included. A hundred years ago there were 13 as well as a brewery. Just as today, part of their trade came from visitors travelling through the town, some of whom stayed overnight. Many of the inns had stabling at their rear, making them the motels of their time. To the residents of Stockbridge the pub was a far more important part of everyday life than today. For most working men it was a nightly routine to go to the pub for a pint, a smoke and a game of some kind.

Their choice began in London Road where the Queen's Head[15] was a long, low thatched building. Part of it was demolished for the construction of Cromer by Charles Simmonds for his son-in-law, Sydney Stares, but Queen's Head Cottage is still present in part of what were the stables and coach house. Next door is May Cottage and the remainder has become the Stockbridge Antiques Centre.

At the bottom of Winton Hill was the Ship Inn (*fig 13*). This was bought in 1911 by two ladies who hated alcohol and it became a temperance hotel

[15] In the source article by F.J. Raggio it is called the King's Head which was the name of John Bucket's inn but there is no doubt that the London Road pub was the Queen's Head. In the 1796-8 directory there were both a King's and a Queen's Head (see Appendix) and a map of that period shows that the King's Head was on the site later occupied by the Grosvenor Hotel.

7 Stockbridge High Street looking east in the early 1900s. The gravelled road surface shows cart tracks; there are piles of manure on the right. The pub on the left is the *Greyhound (courtesy of Edward Roberts)*

(GM). It then became a private home between the wars and the building was later demolished as part of the road-widening for the new road system in the 1970s. Next, between the churchyard and the railway, was the White Hart, still very much in business, having reopened in late April 2000 after extensive renovation. Just over the railway bridge was the Hero, presumably named after Lord Nelson. The building is now Trafalgar House with Hero Cottage next door: the latter was the Stockbridge telephone exchange for a time. Beyond that came the Vine, another flourishing survivor.

Further west along the High Street was the Waggon[16] and Horses, which had earlier been the Red Lion. It is no longer a pub but prospers as Lillie of Stockbridge with its bakery and tearooms. On the other side of the road was the Grosvenor Hotel which, as already noted, replaced the King's Head. In 1900 it was owned by Tom Cannon, the famous jockey. It remains a prominent feature of the High Street and is much used today. Next door was the Hotel Tap, separate from the Grosvenor, which closed in the early 1960s. Beyond the church today is the Stockbridge Peking Restaurant, which a hundred years ago was the Brewery Bar. This closed in 1913.

Opposite the Brewery Bar was the Bell Brewery owned by Mr J Roe of Whitchurch. Next, beyond the Town Hall, was the Wheatsheaf. This later

[16] 'Waggon' was the spelling in common use until the 20th century.

became the Bridge Temperance Hotel which was popular with cyclists. Today it is Broughton Crafts. Further along the Three Cups and the Greyhound, facing each other, are still going strong. The final port of call was over the river and round the corner into Houghton Road, where the Cossack was popular with jockeys and stable lads. It closed in 1966 and is now a private home.

Geoff Merritt points out that in addition to all these public houses there has been a Grenadier in New Street, succeeded by a British Legion hut and that the present pharmacy at one stage was the Angel.

The decline in the number of pubs began when the racing at Danebury Down stopped. It has continued since then for a variety of reasons. Today few country pubs could survive simply by serving men who have spent a day of hard manual labour. Changes in farming, drink-driving laws, television and other entertainments have reduced that trade. Pub profits come as much from providing food as from drink. There is no longer a ban on children and soft drinks are as expensive as alcoholic ones. In the days of the coaching inns, travellers used the stables behind them. Today cars are parked in front of the Stockbridge pubs, thanks to the wide street built to make room for a market, centuries before.

Sources and further reading

Bradbury, Jim (1996) *Stephen and Matilda: The Civil War of 1139-53* Alan Sutton, Stroud. ISBN 0-7509-0612-X

Beresford, Dorothy (1973) *Nether Wallop in Hampshire.* BAS Printers, Nether Wallop. (for details of first horse box and starting gate).

Bonser, K.J. (1970) *The Drovers.* Macmillan and Co. Ltd., London.

Burnfield, Sandy (1999) *Personal communication.*

Cunliffe, Barry (1993) *Danebury* Batsford/English Heritage, London. ISBN 0-7134-6886-6

Dawkins, G.W. (1989) *The Racing Days of Stockbridge* 'Hampshire', p. 47.

Edwards, Bob (1999) *Historic Stockbridge: Archaeological Assessment Document.* Hampshire County Council and English Heritage.

Hill, Rosalind (1976) *A History of Stockbridge.* J.A.C. Publications, Stockbridge.

Hill, Rosalind (1976) *The Manor of Stockbridge.* Proceedings of the Hampshire Field Club and Archaeological Society **32,** p. 93-101.

Hill, Rosalind (1977) *The Borough of Stockbridge.* Proceedings of the Hampshire Field Club and Archaeological Society **33,** pp. 79-88.

Tiller, Kate (1992) *English Local History – An Introduction* Alan Sutton Publishing, Stroud. ISBN 0-86299-958-8

Raggio, F.J. (1969) *Village had 13 pubs – and its own brewery* 'Hampshire', pp. 32-33.

Trevelyan, G.M. (1973) *History of England* Longmans, London.

Webb, K.J. (1979) *The Drovers* 'Hampshire', pp. 39-40.

Other Sources

County Directories: I am grateful to Geoff Merritt for pointing out the value of the county directories, which give a brief picture of each town and village, its location, history and services such as coaches and mail, together with the principal citizens and tradespeople. These directories began in the late 18th century and continued until Kelly's Directory ceased publication in 1939. Some samples are reproduced in the Appendix. They show that until the Second World War Stockbridge had nearly all the trades and services it needed to make it self-sufficient.

Maps: Tithe maps are generally the oldest maps of a community with details of buildings, gardens and fields, their ownership and use. They were drawn up in order to define how much tithe money each property should pay to the rector. The earliest tithe map of Stockbridge in the Hampshire Record Office is dated as 1842. I have also been able to examine, by courtesy of Mr Ray Hill, an earlier map of 1790. This was similar in layout and appearance to subsequent tithe maps, which began in about 1837. This map showed the King's Head Inn at the site later occupied by the Grosvenor Hotel and the Red Lion where the Waggon and Horses later stood.

8 Another early view of the High Street with the date 'Mar 19/04'. There is a cart in the foreground and three boys on bicycles further away. The slope of the railway bridge is well seen at the far end of the street *(courtesy of Jill Harding)*

9 A view of Salisbury Hill, almost certainly during World War I. Not only are there telephone lines, which appeared at about this time, but a soldier in a forage cap can be seen on the right, together with a boy, in front of the fence *(courtesy of Jill Harding)*

4 The Lordship of the Manor and the Courts Baron and Leet

Each year, most often in March, a very unusual ceremony takes place in the upper floor of Stockbridge Town Hall. It has been dated at least to the 12th century and it has its roots in the feudal system which allowed grazing rights on common land to freemen of the Borough, the burgesses, and to the tenants of the Lord of the Manor. The burgesses and the tenants would meet each year with the Lord of the Manor, or his representative, the Steward. The purpose was to confirm and record their rights to graze and to hunt on these lands and to agree the periods in which these rights would be exercised. Another function was to try those accused of crimes. A shortened version of the Lord of the Manor's address of March 2000, explaining more about these courts, is given in the Appendix. In the mediæval period the courts, the Court Baron for the burgesses and the Court Leet for the tenants, would have been full of tension, with disagreement, debate and punishment. Today the ceremony is enjoyed by all participants and it helps to reinforce the community spirit of Stockbridge. There are numerous other Lords of the Manor in England but in hardly any of these Lordships does this ceremony survive. How does it come about that it still exists almost uniquely in this town?

To answer this we have to go back to the 19th century. In 1824 Joseph Foster Barham, who had been MP for the borough, bought the Lordship of the Manor from the Duchy of Lancaster. Subsequently it was sold from one owner to another, but all this time the court meetings survived. It was accepted that the lordship of the manor gave the 'ownership' of Stockbridge Down and the Common Marsh, though in the tithe map of 1842 the owners are given as 'owners of land in the parish of Stockbridge'. In 1890 the Lord of the Manor, a man named Lancashire, tried to deny the citizens of Stockbridge their right of access to and recreation on the Down: in effect he wanted to take full possession of it. The burgesses fought the case all the way to the House of Lords and won. The bankrupted Lancashire, in disgust, sold the lordship to a London pawnbroker and the courts were discontinued.

In 1920 the lordship was transferred to Sir Norman Hill, Bt. who was both a lawyer and a keen amateur historian. There were still residents who knew the traditional form of the proceedings and he was able to reinstate the courts in 1921. The mace, seal and staff, which had been preserved by the previous steward, Mr Cawley, were restored. Once more the courts were in session and they have been held annually since then, with some extra meetings for matters of special interest.

In 1944, Sir Norman died and shortly afterwards Dr Gray Hill, Sir Norman's eldest son, and by then the second baronet, was killed in action. The lordship passed to his sister, Professor Rosalind Hill, herself a distinguished historian and a chronicler of Stockbridge's history. She decided to give the lands, Stockbridge Down and the Common Marsh, to the National Trust but continued to act as Lady of the Manor until her death in 1997. Since then the Lord of the Manor has been Mr Christopher Robathan, the former Steward.

The National Trust owns and has overall control of these lands but has enthusiastically supported the continuation of the lordship and the Courts Baron and Leet. In fact National Trust representatives take part in the annual ceremony. You may picture the hall, packed with Stockbridge residents, when the Court Crier and Bailiff comes to the door and asks the audience to stand for the entrance of the Lord of the Manor and his Steward, robed in gowns, with representatives of the National Trust and any distinguished guests, such as the Mayor of Test Valley. They file in to take their places and then the Lord of the Manor starts by asking,

"Mr Crier, would you please proclaim the court?"

The Crier rings his bell[17] and calls, "Oyez, oyez, oyez; all manner of persons who do owe suit or favour of these courts, draw near and give your attention, answering everyone to his name or pay your fines. God bless the Queen and the Lords of all Manors."

Next the Lord of the Manor asks, "Mr Steward, would you please appoint the jurors and name their foreman?"

The Steward reads out the names of the selected jurors, nine for the Court Leet and six for the Court Baron and they take their places at the side of the hall. He asks them to appoint their foreman. Next, the foreman and then the whole jury take the oath. As the foreman stands with upraised

[17] The bell is inscribed 'Borough of Stockbrige. C. Bishop, Baileff, 1786' Subsequently a 'd' has been added to correct the spelling.

hand, the Steward says, "You shall well and truly enquire and true presentment make of all such articles, matters and things as shall be given you in charge. The Queen's counsel, your companions' and your own you shall keep secret and undisclosed. You shall present no man for envy, hatred or malice nor spare any man for fear, favour or affection or any hope of reward, but according to the best of your knowledge and the information you receive, you shall present the truth, the whole truth and nothing but the truth. I invite you to say 'I swear'."

The foreman and jury being sworn in, the Lord of the Manor then addresses them, "Burgesses of the borough and tenants of the Manor of Stockbridge, I have caused these courts to be assembled in accordance with our ancient traditions in order that you may choose your officers for the coming year and present any matter touching the affairs of the borough and manor which you think that these courts should consider."

The Lord of the Manor then goes on, first to 'record with affection' the names of those burgesses, i.e. citizens of Stockbridge, who have died in the previous year. This is followed by a review of matters and events of general interest which have occurred in Stockbridge during the year. The jury are then asked to 'consider your findings and present fit and proper persons to serve in the office of Bailiff, of Sergeant-at-Mace and Hayward for the coming year'.

The functions of the court officers are mainly ceremonial but the Hayward still has some of the duties which he would have had in ancient times. A hayward herded the common cattle of a town and had charge of the fences and enclosures, being responsible for preventing the cattle from breaking through them. In collaboration with the National Trust he still has such functions.

While the jury is out the Lord of the Manor may give a further address and then the public are able to admire the fine silver mace and seal, both given to the borough in 1681 as a bribe or inducement to vote for one Essex Strode. The beautifully decorated staff of the Hayward, which also dates from the 17th century, is also on display.

When the jury returns, the foreman announces the name of the Bailiff and Crier, the Sergeant-at-Mace and the Hayward for the coming year. The Hayward's decision on the dates for the opening and closure of grazing on the Marsh may also be announced, together with the numbers of cattle and horses which will be allowed. Sometimes this decision is delayed if the weather has made the ground too soft. Those who graze their animals or who shoot on the Down pay for this and the proceeds go to causes within the town, such as the church or recreation ground.

This stage is followed by remarks by the National Trust representative, who reviews the issues and problems of the year. For example, on the Down the lack of regular grazing has allowed scrub and bushes to develop, while a recurrent problem on the Marsh and the Down is the growth of ragwort. This is a weed poisonous to horses and cattle, and the Trust promotes a ragwort 'pull' each July. More recently careful spraying of thistles has been allowed, in order to preserve the quality of the grassland on the Marsh.

Finally the officers are sworn in. (The officers serving in 2000 are Steward, Gavin Burnett; Bailiff, David Webster; Sergeant-at-Mace, Ray Standfield; Hayward, John Wrayton.) The Bailiff is given charge of the seal, the Sergeant-at-Mace has custody of the mace and the Hayward has the Hayward Staff for the ensuing year. Then the courts are closed.

In her addresses to the courts, Professor Rosalind Hill often stressed the toughness, independence of mind and community spirit of the people of Stockbridge. The persistence of this ceremonial is a tribute to these qualities but it is equally due to the vision, generosity of spirit and affection for Stockbridge which she and her father showed. It is also due to the enlightened attitude of the National Trust, who having become owners of 233 acres of common land, encouraged the co-operative administration of their new territory in such a way that Stockbridge can feel that it is genuinely involved in its maintenance. However, it has to be said that in July 1999 only two of the volunteer force taking part in the back-aching task of pulling ragwort on the Common Marsh actually came from Stockbridge. The ragwort 'pull' on Stockbridge Down in July 2000 drew five locals among the 14 volunteers.

10 The High Street in about 1914 looking east. Telegraph poles have now been installed. The slope at the far end of the street is the railway bridge *(courtesy of Edward Roberts)*

11 The High Street looking east, 2000

12 Looking eastward from the railway bridge in the early 1900s. The white post seen above the left side
of the bridge is also seen in figure 13 in front of the Ship Inn.

13 The bottom of Winton Hill in the early 1900s. In about 1972, the Ship Inn, by then a private house,
was demolished to make room for the new road system. Before that tiles on the roof corner were
regularly knocked off by double decker buses (LS).

5 The Twentieth Century

*...cars were so rare that...children would come out of
the house to see one pass.*

STOCKBRIDGE BETWEEN THE WARS

There are no direct recollections of life in the town before the First World War but a number of our illustrations, *(figs 7, 8, 9, 10, 12, 13, 14, 15, 16)* show how it looked. However, many people can recall life in the town in the Twenties and this makes a convenient point at which to start.

At the end of the First World War Stockbridge was still a small, quiet market town. Cattle, pigs and sheep were sold each week in the market area behind what is still the Market Room in the Grosvenor Hotel. Market Day brought 'flies and fleas and dust' to the town. At the time the streets were partly cobbled and cars were so rare that, as Monica Harding recalled, children would come out of their houses to see one pass. Stockbridge had a railway station connecting it to Andover and Romsey and to other villages in the Test valley. The main sources of employment, other than farming, were Bradfield's Mill, now part of Longstock Mill, a private home, and the racing stables.

The town had, as can be seen in the Appendix, a large range of shops and other services which made it almost self-sufficient. It had a Fire Brigade, whose pump was horse-drawn and manned by volunteers. Laurie Stares, whose father was the second Captain of the Brigade, recalls that when there was news of a fire a man or a boy was sent down to the Common Marsh to collect the horse, unless the fire was in the High Street, when the crew would be able to pull the pump there themselves. The pump was kept behind the Vine Public House and another man was told to make sure that a pin[18] of beer was ready in the pub; this was the only 'payment' the team received! Floods overflowing into the High Street were a regular occurrence and this continued until the main Test bridge was rebuilt in 1963.

All these details come from the recollections of those who lived in

[18] A 'pin' is a cask of 4 ½ gallons.

14 The High Street, probably in about 1914, looking west from the railway bridge. Fig 1 is the nearest modern equivalent *(courtesy of Derek Tempero)*

15 Street looking west in the early 1900s. The view is taken from between the Grosvenor Hotel and St Peter's Church *(courtesy of Edward Roberts)*

Stockbridge in the 1920s and 30s. It is time to introduce them and their memories, which are combined in this chapter.

Monica Harding

Mrs Harding who, sadly, died on June 5, 2000, grew up in the town and became a teacher in the Stockbridge Primary School from 1938 to 1943, when her first child was born. She wrote her memories in a charming book *Remembering Stockbridge and the Primary School from 1920 to 1960*. She also wrote *Thank you for Stockbridge*, a book of verses, composed while convalescing from an illness. It too recalls the life and people of the town before, during and after the Second World War. *This and That: Memories and Reflections* is a further book of verse, published in 1997. Even when she was frail and infirm, she radiated a bright-eyed goodness of spirit and continued to be a moving force in the Baptist Chapel. When she spoke about Stockbridge she was full of gratitude for the enjoyment of past days, coupled with a ready acceptance of the changes which have made the town so different today. We start with her early memories of Stockbridge, taken, by kind permission, from 'Remembering Stockbridge'.

'I came to Stockbridge as a four-year-old child in 1920. My father, Henry Stratton, came to take over a Provision Merchant and Baker's shop on the premises now used as Post Office and Grocery Store; also the adjoining shop, now Broughton Crafts. At the rear of the present Post Office was a large Bake house and behind that, stables. In those days, bread and groceries were delivered by horse wagon or by an errand boy on his bicycle.

'When we arrived in Stockbridge there were few modern amenities. We had no electricity, no mains water, no sewerage, and no tarmacadamed street. The sides of the High Street were cobbled up to the highway in the middle. Lighting was oil lamps or candles; heating was coal, wood or oil; and water came from the river, collected in buckets, or from wells or bore holes. Waste matter went into cess pits or the river or onto the gardens. Toilets were for the most part earth closets at the bottom of the gardens – sometimes called 'Privies'. These were cleared and the contents buried by a member of the household, or emptied and removed by the local 'Bogman' in his cart.

'There were few cars and one seldom saw an aeroplane. Transport was the railway – the 'Sprat and Winkle' line – running between Andover and

16 A picture of Salisbury Hill, taken from the old bridge in the early 1900s. The sheds in the foreground on the right have since been demolished *(courtesy of Edward Roberts)*

17 Salisbury Hill, 2000

Romsey and then on to Southampton via Redbridge. Apart from this there were bicycles, the occasional car, plus a few carts and pony traps and an early open charabanc which had a hood to put up if it rained. For the most part, local people used 'Shanks's pony'!

'In the early 1920s there were three places of worship: Church of England, Baptist and Methodist but the latter very soon closed down. Around the churches much of the social life of the village revolved. There were also seven public houses including the Grosvenor Hotel.

'Within easy reach of the village were two flourishing racing stables, Atty Persse at Chattis Hill and Mr Easterbee, a short way up Winton Hill. Two, and at one time three blacksmiths were usually kept fully employed.

'In the High Street were at least four grocers, four butchers, a couple of builders, who were also undertakers, two drapers and a very good ironmonger. The village also boasted three cobblers, a saddler, upholsterer, a newsagent, several sweetshops, a plumber, a laundry and also several washer women. There was a busy Post Office, a railway station with several sidings. Three milkmen (if my memory is correct) delivered daily using hand or horse pulled milk carts. They measured out pints of 'unpasteurised' into our waiting jug or can.

'Also there was Moley Willis[19], who trapped moles on the downs and marsh, and Mossy Green who collected moss in his little cart to sell for lining graves[20] – the old bowler hat that he wore was almost as green as his moss.

'One character of real note was known to all as 'Old Dollar': he was the Town Crier[21]. Dressed in top-hat and black morning coat with a Union Jack gracing the front of his body, he walked up and down the street, ringing his bell and crying the news. I last remember him shouting news of the General Strike in 1926 when there were no newspapers, no post and no trains and only a few folk had their own telephone or wireless. Because of the difficulty of coal delivery at this time, a number of people bought peat, cut on the marsh, to use as fuel.

'Today the village population numbers around five hundred and fifty but in the 1920s it was well over a thousand. Much larger families dwelt in

[19] Also known as 'Bumper' Willis because he flattened molehills on the gallops on Stockbridge Down, using a large board mounted on a broom handle.
[20] And for the floral trade in London.
[21] His name was Edgar Dollar but when asked by the young Laurie Stares why he was called 'Old Dollar he answered 'because 'I do 'oller'.

many of the houses and cottages. In fact, many of the cottages have been demolished and larger but fewer houses have been built on sites such as Nelson Close, Trafalgar Way and Blandford Row. Other houses which were in the High Street no longer exist. On the left hand side of the road leading to Romsey, opposite Old St Peter's Church and next to the small cemetery at the end of East End Cottages, was a driveway which led up and round a beautifully kept lawn, to the Union or Workhouse. Here lived a number of homeless people including children, and Casual Wards housed many a tramp for a night.'

The Workhouse

Both as a schoolgirl and later as a teacher Mrs Harding felt sorry for the workhouse children in their coarse beige holland cloth uniforms. The Workhouse was run by a Board of Guardians and had a resident manager. Its inhabitants included tramps and vagrants and some who were then called mentally handicapped. Able bodied residents were expected to work. Those who had any money had to contribute to their keep. Some tramps therefore buried their money in the banks opposite to avoid having to pay[22]. The Workhouse closed after the end of the Second World War.

This building, constructed in 1837 and designed for up to 150 inhabitants might have been thought to have been an asset which would find some other use. For a time it was used both by the primary and secondary modern schools. The ground floor had Domestic Science for girls and in the first the boys did woodwork while Rural Science was taught in the gardens. But eventually it was demolished and the site is now full of trees.

Laurie Stares

To many people Laurie Stares is 'Mr Stockbridge'. His grandfather came to Stockbridge in 1897. Both his grandparents lived in the town. Laurie grew up in Stockbridge, going first to the Primary School and then, at fourteen, for two years to the Portsmouth Municipal College which had been evacuated to Longstock and Leckford. For eighteen months he worked for Rank's Flour Mills in Sutton Scotney[23] and then reached the age to do his National Service, when he was commissioned in the Hampshire Regiment.

[22] This may explain why in the early 1900s the building now occupied by Diligence was a tramps' dosshouse, the tramps sleeping on straw (LS).
[23] The mill in Southampton had been 'blitzed'. Laurie cycled to Sutton Scotney from Stockbridge every day.

Most of his service was on the Austrian-Yugoslav border where the duties were mainly to control smuggling and to restore normal services in the area.

In 1948 he returned to work for Rank's and the rest of his working life was spent in the corn trade. He rose within Rank's to become a wheat buyer, buying from corn merchants. He stayed in this post for 20 years. Then, in 1973, his expertise led him to be asked to work for a corn merchant, buying and selling grain. In this phase of his life he worked in all for three companies, travelling widely in the south of England and building up a range of contacts among people who were 'commercial enemies but personal friends'. He retired in 1989.

It is no surprise that someone who worked so hard as a boy is still busy. He has contributed to the Stockbridge community in countless ways. From the age of seven he has been, with a few interruptions, a regular member of the church choir and has been active in church matters for many years. He served as Clerk to the Parish Council from 1972 to 1994. He was Chairman of the Town Hall Committee from 1991 to 1996 . He was Crier and Bailiff to the Courts Baron and Leet from 1979 to 1998. Until the end of 1999 he was involved in running a Monday Luncheon Club for the elderly. He has many memories of life in the town since his boyhood which are recorded in this chapter.

A Butcher's Boy, Part-Time

...dressed in his white flannels he was asked to 'just hold this pig while I stick it'. Blood went everywhere...

In 1897 his grandfather bought the shop now occupied by Folklore *(fig 18)*. Animals were led to be slaughtered through the space between the shop and Victoria Cottage. The business later moved to the premises, now Diligence, which were then a doss-house for vagrants, together with Providence House, next door. His son Sydney, Laurie's father, became apprenticed to a butcher in Whitchurch and then joined his father. In 1903 Mr Stares bought 10 acres behind his house and shop. When Laurie's father Sydney took over he worked hard to build up the business both as a butchery and a dairy. Twenty cows were kept and milked daily. As a boy of six Laurie was already delivering milk to customers on his bike, in cans, two or three to a handlebar.

Nearly all the meat came from local farms or the Stares' own pigs. Before

18 The Christmas display at the Stares' butchers' shop in the early 1900s. Cattle and sheep were led through the small doorway on the right of the picture to be slaughtered on the premises. This shop is now 'Folklore'.

the first War cattle and sheep might be purchased in Winchester and driven on foot to Stockbridge via Farley Mount along the drove roads still in existence. This was a journey of 12-13 miles taking 3-4 hours. By the 1920s his father had a van and most stock were moved by cattle lorry. The normal routine would be to purchase a bullock on Monday and keep it on water only till the afternoon of Wednesday, which was early closing day. Then it would be slaughtered, cut in half and hung. It was sprinkled with pepper to deter flies and kept until the following Monday, when it would be quartered and jointed and the joints put in the ice box. This was the only practical means of refrigeration until the first refrigerator was bought in the late 1930s. Laurie was often sent with the carrier bike to the station to collect a delivery of a hundredweight of ice. This would then be broken up for use in the boxes.

Another of his jobs was to prepare the intestines of slaughtered animals, removing fat to provide chitterlings and washing through the intestines, which could then be sold for manufacture into sausage skins. He would also stoke the fire under the huge copper bowl in which pig carcasses were scalded to remove their hair. He would help roll up the hides of sheep after they had been sprinkled with salt and pepper to deter flies. Killing

19 The modern equivalent – the butchers John Robinson's. On the right of the picture are Miss Elizabeth Viney's antique shop and Groves' newsagents.

pigs was always exciting and often messy. On the day he was first due to play for the school cricket XI, dressed in his white flannels, he was asked to 'just hold this pig while I stick it'. Blood went everywhere and he had to play the match in grey flannels!

In those days it was said that you could 'eat every part of the pig except its squeal' and the Stares' family diet often included elements such as kidney, liver, heart or trotters which had not been sold. The heads of pigs, sheep or calves were particular delicacies, providing brains, tongue and the meat which could be picked off. Each head had its own special flavour, each 'a gorgeous taste'.

On Saturdays his work began at 8.0 a.m., cycling with a brim-full basket to Longstock, where he delivered from Test Cottage up to Longstock Park. This done, a second round took in lower Longstock and South Side Cottages. Saturday afternoon's work was the week's clean-up, boiling all utensils in hot water and scrubbing boards and tables till they were white, free of any blood stains. For all this work he was paid 2/6d[24], which made him rich compared to other boys.

Laurie also tells of the competition in the trade. Before the First World War Bill Corrall began by pushing a barrow of meat from Andover to Stockbridge on Saturdays and selling from the barrow outside what is now

[24] Approximately £4 at 1999 prices. Today's paper 'boys' in Stockbridge can earn over £20 a week though this partly reflects the shortage of suitable candidates and the way in which parental affluence can undermine youthful enterprise.

the Co-op. After a time he moved to the premises now occupied by Sykes, the greengrocers. His son, Jim, took over and as the business prospered he started as a fishmonger in that shop and moved the butcher's shop to nearby premises. Ultimately he sold the business to John Robinson who has built it up into one of the most successful butchers' shops in the south of England *(fig 19)*. As Laurie himself was not interested in taking over the family firm, his father sold his business on retirement and until 1997 it was run by two of his employees.

Making Your Own Entertainment

Between the wars few people travelled. Apart from the radio, there was no entertainment unless you made it for yourself. Children could play in Marsh Court Road riding bicycles or making tree houses with no interruption from cars or people. They might also play on the Common Marsh, undisturbed all day amid lapwing, redshank and skylarks. At Marsh Court itself, then kept immaculate by ten or twelve gardeners, there was a yearly party for the Sunday School, with tea and a chance to play in the grounds. Formal entertainments for adults and children were mostly based at the Town Hall and various local characters contributed. Sam Carey, chauffeur-gardener at Hermit Lodge, who lived in Drover's House, sang and told jokes at such parties. Charlie Lee and Billy Chalk did a double act at the piano, singing verses about topical events, with a chorus which ended 'And the Vicar and I will be there'. Fred Shadwell, a farmer from Wallop, would dress as a 'yokel' in smock, red kerchief and felt hat and would deliver yarn after yarn, often in fairly coarse language. The character of the milder stories may be judged by the following interchange between the bailiff of a farm and Georgy a young apprentice:

Bailiff: *'Georgy who was that little maiden I see thee with the other night?'*
Georgy: *'Why sir, that was Mary, the new maid up at the Squire's.'*
Bailiff: *'Oh, be ye courting, Georgy?'*
Georgy: *'Yessir, we be courting.'*
Bailiff: *'Have 'ee kissed her, Georgy?'*
Georgy: *'Oh yessir.'*
Bailiff: *'Whereabouts have 'ee kissed her, Georgy?'*
Georgy: *'Well sir, I don't rightly know but we had the radio on and it was somewhere between the Fatstock Prices and the Children's Hour.'*

Jack East, who had a photographic memory, could recite long passages from Dickens' 'Christmas Carol', while Mr Stratton, Monica Harding's father, gave monologues which were a mixture of songs and poems that he composed himself.

All this may seem rather unsophisticated to a generation used to television and other modern entertainments, yet it was part of what held the village together. Most people lived, worked, shopped and socialised in the village: their life *was* the village. As a result there was a strong community spirit. It was vigorously expressed in support for the football XI at their matches. This could result in fights with opposing supporters when feelings ran high.

Laurie's Postscript

'In 1953 I was fortunate to have my own house built and it has been an enormous privilege to live among and work for the community into which I was born. One of my greatest regrets is that today Stockbridge children are unable to enjoy the continuity which I experienced. Property values are out of reach of all young people when they marry and want to settle down. They have to migrate to cheaper accommodation in the towns.'

Hubert (Bert) Earney

Some children walked two miles, some up to six. Most had only one pair of boots.

Hubert Earney was born in 1920 and brought up in Stockbridge, leaving it to begin his military service in 1939. After the War he began work as a journalist on the Southern Daily Echo, with a particular interest in local news. He has written a number of articles about life in Stockbridge and retains a warm and affectionate interest in the town. He retired in 1985 and lives in Andover. His portrait adds detail to the picture of pre-war life here, in particular by showing how different the shops were in that period.

'Although I left Stockbridge in 1939 I still look back on the town with great affection. My childhood was a happy one and even now a stroll down the High Street finds it basically much the same as it was in those far off days. The verges are no longer gravelly and unpaved: you cannot kick a ball up the High Street as we often did in the 20s and early 30s. But apart from the surfaces, and from additions such as telephone kiosks and street lighting, it bears a strong similarity to its aspect in the 1920s, *(fig 20)*.

20 A photograph, probably from the early 1930s, showing the High Street looking west from a point level with the Vine Inn. The car is parked outside Lloyds Bank, which then occupied the front room of Frank Wiltshire's home, next door to his bakery. Since the Second World War this building has been occupied by the Co-op. The awning is over Whiffen's newsagents and tobacconists. The number of lines on the telegraph poles has greatly increased compared with Fig 10. There are no pavements and only the middle of the road is tarmacked *(courtesy of Mrs Marjorie Butler – née Wiltshire)*

'In fact we had many outlets for our recreation and amusement – the Marsh, the Common Down, Marshcourt Road and Little Dean. With these four play areas we were never bored for a moment, even though (perhaps because) there was no TV, no cinema in the town and few radios. For the 'movies' we had to go to Andover or Winchester or wait for the twice-yearly visit of 'Pettits Popular Pictures'. Mr Pettit, a retired actor with his dog as his constant companion, showed 'talkies' in the Town Hall, for an entrance fee of about 3d or 6d. His shows usually consisted of Charlie Chaplin or Harold Lloyd comedies but I remember that he once showed a thriller called 'The Cat Creeps'. Most of the population of the borough were afraid to venture out at night on their own for weeks afterwards!

'Little Dean, home of Stockbridge FC for more than 60 years has now disappeared, though its name has been adopted by the nursing home on Winton Hill. The football pitch was a gift to the town of Sir Norman Hill when he became Lord of the Manor. It lay to the east of the railway line and north of the railway station, *(fig 25)* and most of the site has been taken up by the new roundabout where the A30 joins the A3057. It had a pronounced slope in one corner[25] and we boys reckoned that the slope was as good as a couple of goals start to the home side!

'The Common Marsh gave us paddling and tiddler catching and learning to swim in the 'Big Hole' with the aid of a rubber inner tube. Before the First World War an attempt had been made to lay a cricket pitch on the Marsh. The 'table' sank in the marshy subsoil but the square which was left was good enough for us youngsters to play on.

'Nearby was Marshcourt Road, whose thick vegetation was ideal for birds-nesting, making huts and camps from the branches and playing hide and seek, cowboys and Indians, cavaliers and roundheads or what you will. And what Stockbridge boy did not get his first awareness of the opposite sex in one or other of these locations?

'Further down the road the slopes of the King's Somborne bank were steep enough to make them ideal for tobogganing in winter; in those days there always seemed to be enough snow[26]. In summer the slopes did equally well for the buggies we made from old boxes with pram wheels retrieved from the 'dump' on the Leckford Road.

'Many other games took place as we walked to and from the village school in London Road. Conkers, hopscotch, tops, hoops, bows and arrows would all have their season. There were no school buses and some children walked fair distances; two miles was not uncommon and some walked up to six. Most had only one pair of boots so when they wore out the owner would be absent from school until they were repaired.'

A Boy's-Eye View of the High Street

Bethel would always oblige a lad who wanted a burst football case mended or a split cricket bat bound with twine.

'The visitor to Stockbridge today would be forgiven for taking the view that it is merely a tourist town of antique shops, refreshment houses and gift shops. In the 20s there was a diversity of trades and services which made the town almost self-sufficient: you could buy almost anything there. Stockbridge had its own blacksmith, saddler and barber; it had four cobblers, three dairies, three butchers, two bakers, two grocers, a greengrocer, a draper, five confectioners and three garages-cum-filling

[25] Still visible in the small field to the south-east of the roundabout.
[26] These banks are now overgrown with scrub which was able to thrive when myxomatosis killed most of the rabbit population.

stations, one of which also offered the sale, repair and hire of bicycles (1d an hour). There were three builders, two also acting as undertakers[27].

'To look in more detail let us imagine a boy walking the High Street, and looking at the shops and other places with a special interest for him. He starts along the south side of the street, beginning at the Winchester end (today's equivalents are shown in brackets). The first shop (*Terra Firma Tiles and Jonathan Shirley Antiques*) he looked at was the grocery and provisions merchants of Thos G. Tabor. Tommy Tabor was a cheerful chap who ran the business for about 40 years, assisted by his wife and their daughter Edna. Everything in the shop was on open display but there were no reports of anyone being harmed by his wares. (Did we accept the odd upset tummy as a fact of life or were we immunised by many 'pecks of dirt'?).

'Corralls, first of three butchers (*John Robinson's*) was another essentially family business run by old Mr Corrall, his son Jim, also known as Billy, and his sister-in-law, Miss Lunn. She always wore a large butcher's apron and a man's flat cap and my, didn't she work! Next door, (*Elizabeth Viney Antiques*) was the fascinating saddler's shop of Bethel Jacob. There were then plenty of horses around to ensure a good trade for Bethel and his assistant Bill Kimble, but with all his commitments Bethel would always oblige a lad who wanted a burst football case mended or a split cricket bat bound with twine. And I don't think he ever charged more than a tanner (2½p) for these services. After that (*Groves' newsagents*) was Mr Orpwood's sweetshop, a mecca for kids. It was a shop to be visited warily, for on the counter was an 'electric shock' machine. You put a penny in and turned a handle while holding a knob and the machine sent a buzz up your arm. Old 'Orpie' who had a sadistic turn of humour, loved nothing better than to hold a youngster's fingers round its handles so you couldn't let go: the old devil would laugh his head off while you yelled for mercy.

'Then came the opening to Prospect Place with, behind it, the blacksmith's forge of Mr George Berriman, another emporium which attracted we kids like a magnet. George was the embodiment of Longfellow's smith – white hair, white moustache, twinkling eyes, the muscles of his brawny arms as 'strong as iron bands'. If you behaved he would let you watch while a horse was shod or a horseshoe forged – first

[27] Some of these figures differ from those in Monica Harding's account.

heated in the flames and then shaped on the anvil. But more practically he would mend, for about 3d, the iron hoops which we boys used to trundle along the roads. From time to time they would snap at a joint. George used to re-weld them in the forge and off we would go, 'mobile' again and trundling happily.

'Past the stream were the Stockbridge Butchers (*Diligence*), run by the Stares family for all of 70 years. Then, next to their home in Providence House (*For Goodness' Sake*) was the little shop of 'Barber' Miles who tended to the tonsorial needs of the men and boys of Stockbridge (*George Clark*). 'Barber' Brown took over when Mr Miles retired in the mid-thirties: when he stopped it was many years before there was a hairdresser in the town.

'The first local bus company was run by a Mr Prebble who owned the Grosvenor Garage (*Stockbridge Racing*). He had an old De Dion Bouton with a bonnet shaped like a cocoa tin; this was the town's first bus. Among its regular commissions, it conveyed the local football team to away matches and many was the time when the players had to get out and push, especially when climbing Conholt Hill on the way home from Vernham Dean. Incidentally, the first car owner was Dr W.K. Loveless, one of three generations of local GPs in the parish. He lived at Steepleton but his car could not get up Somborne Hill in first gear and his chauffeur, Sid Gibbs, had to put it into reverse and go up backwards!

'A second garage near to Prebbles was the County Garage, run by Mr Frank Higgin while his wife ran a confectionery next door. The garage and the shop continued under other owners after the War but were later demolished to make way for the homes in Wessex Mews.

'Next door, at London House, (*the Wykeham Galleries*), was the drapers shop of Mr Charlie Hale, where you could buy almost anything in the haberdashery line from a reel of cotton to a new three-piece suit. At the back Mr Hale also operated a boot and shoe repair business through his employee, George Diaper. It was one of four cobblers in the town then, the others being Alfie Dumper further down the street on the opposite side and Bert Taylor and Mr Lovelock both in the London Road (now the Old London Road).

'The next set of shops came after the Town Hall bridge at Bridge House (*Orvis*) where there was a large grocery and drapers belonging to Mr Henry George Stratton, father to Monica Harding. He was a dear old gentleman and his humorous monologues were a wow at local concerts. The Wheatsheaf Temperance Hotel came next (*Broughton Crafts*) and then came the bakery and shop of Mr W.G. Cox (*Londis Stores and Post Office*). I can still smell his freshly baked buns in my mind's nose!

'His establishment stood at the head of Blandford Row, then a street of seven houses, six of them small cottages with, at the end, a larger house, occupied by my maternal grandfather, Mr Arthur Wyndham North, known to all as 'Jasper'. With his wife and their three daughters and four sons he ran a small farm and operated one of the three dairy rounds in Stockbridge, the milk being supplied from their own cows. The story goes that one day on his rounds with pony and milk float, he heard that a milk inspector was approaching. Jasper's whip was smartly applied to the pony's flank which made it shy. The cart tipped, spilling the churn of milk onto the street and when Jasper met the inspector he lamented that a wonderful drop of milk had been lost. "I do wish you could have sampled it".

'What was then the home and builders office of Mr Herbert Fowgies, has now reverted to use as a pub, the 'Three Cups'. Beyond it was a sweet shop (*Folklore*) run by a very handsome widow, Mrs Mowatt, and her extremely pretty daughter, Lilla. All the boys in the town fancied getting to know Lilla but none, so far as I know, got beyond 'first base'.

'A few doors on (*Queensland*) was Jack Farwell's dairy and opposite it was Mr Ted Jeanes' sweet shop and ice cream parlour (*Brockman's*). The sweets were mostly contained in large glass jars, as was the practice at that time. The ice creams were delicious and Ted had a tricycle and rode it for miles around selling them: this was long before Walls thought of the idea.

'As now, the next cluster of shops were some way on. First (*Trout Cottage*) came the greengrocery and game merchant's run by 'Doughy' Kent, a big man with a beard. A loveable scamp, he ran an annual 'draw' at Christmas. It was rumoured that he put pins through the tickets of family and close friends so that when rummaging through the bag his finger would be pricked by a pin. It was then a simple matter to release the pin and draw out the winning ticket. His neighbour, Herbert Jerome, was a butcher (*Stockbridge Pharmacy*) whose speciality was faggots. I am not a faggot lover but their aroma was delightful and it was said that as you ate them the gravy ran down your chin.

'Then came Cozens (*Robjents*), stationers, confectioners and

21 An early view of Wiltshire's bakery, before 1919 when Lloyds Bank occupied the front room on the right. Home delivery of bread by bicycle or horse-drawn cart was usual at the time *(courtesy of Mrs Marjorie Butler)*

tobacconists, a most pleasant shop run by a most pleasant family. Alongside it was another of the centres of attraction to which we boys were invariably drawn, Parker's garage (*Stokes' garage*). This was a garage, filling station, cycle shop, radio store; whatever you could think of, he had it. Tom Parker was an ingenious man full of new ideas. At first he sold petrol in two gallon cans, delivered to his customers in a motor-bike and side-car. He was the first to sell radios in Stockbridge. He recharged the accumulators which powered those old radios by building a water-wheel in an outhouse over the stream which passed the house. This generated the electricity which gave expired batteries their new charge. His sons, Jack, Jim and Tony were my special pals and we spent many happy hours in Parker's meadow or swimming in the stream. It was in Parker's shop I heard my first radio broadcast, the 1929 Cup Final in which Portsmouth were beaten 1-2 by Bolton Wanderers.

'Further east one came to Snelgrove's Dairy[28] (*Stockbridge Peking*) and then St Peter's Church and the Grosvenor Hotel. In the 1920s the annual Sheep Fair was still held and on July 10th each year we boys would delight

[28] Laurie Stares adds: 'Bert Snelgrove was an avid smoker and was able to keep the ash on his cigarette until it started to singe his beard. The talking point in the village was that the ash only fell off when he bent down to ladle a pint into his customer's can or jug. When this was complained about his answer was invariably 'Oh, that's potash; it's good for you'.

in getting up early to help (?) drive the sheep into the fairground pens behind the hotel.

'The Post Office at that time and until the 1970s was just to the east of the Waggon and Horses bridge (*the Frame Shop*). It was kept by a Mr Hickman, the first man I saw with a glass eye. He and his family lived over the shop, as indeed did most of the shopkeepers in those days. Just over the next bridge was Wiltshire's shop and bakery (*the Co-op; figs 20 and 21*). I remember his currant buns with particular pleasure. And then came the newsagent Mr Cyril Whiffen[29]. I made a beeline there every Wednesday and Saturday to buy the 'Gem' and the 'Magnet', to devour the stories of Billy Bunter, Tom Merry, Arthur Augustus D'Arcy and many others. The last shop in the street was that of Frank Lane, Stockbridge's only ironmonger (*Lane's Antiques*) as well as toy shop, who was usually among the first traders to stock fireworks as November 5th approached.

'So ends the tour of the High Street of the beloved town of my boyhood. Full of life, full of friends, full of characters; a wonderful place in which to grow up.'

---

[29] At that stage Mr Whiffen was working from his home. He later took over the newsagent's business across the road, now A E Groves.

STOCKBRIDGE IN THE WAR

The Second World War affected Stockbridge in much the same way as countless other villages and country towns. Men of the age for military service went away and older men, women and teenagers had to carry on, working farms, shops and other businesses as best they could. Children from the cities came as evacuees to escape the expected bombs. Streets were dark at night due to the 'blackout' which was monitored by air raid wardens. Once the air attacks began, from 1940 onwards, there were frequent raids on Portsmouth and Southampton. The only bomb damage in Stockbridge was two craters still visible in the middle of the Common Marsh and a further bomb on the north side of the town.

Food was rationed and coupons were needed for items such as meat, bacon, eggs, butter, sugar, tea and, of course, sweets. In the countryside this restriction was usually less severe because there were often a few extra eggs or some pig, chicken or rabbit meat to be had. Coupons were also needed for clothing and even for fabrics. As a result clothing became rather dull: or a little unusual as when a skirt was made from a tablecloth or curtain material. Beyond these general changes there were some particular ones.

Evacuees

...a knock on the door. 'Please Mrs Stratton, can I be your evacuee?'
'When term started I think I had over fifty five and six year-olds.'
... a bucket and seat as a makeshift toilet... everyone wanted 'TO GO'!

Monica Harding gives a vivid picture of the arrival of evacuees. By the outbreak of war she was a teacher in the village school, now the Primary School. Evacuation of children from the big cities actually began before the outbreak of war on September 3rd. On the 31st August, the school was ready:

'The classroom at the north end of the school, normally used for woodwork, was cleared for use by the doctor and nurse and others doing administrative work. We were expecting children from Flying Bull Lane School, Portsmouth, a secondary school, and also mothers and babies from the same area. They trailed up from the station where they had arrived and into the school – such a forlorn group.

'Brothers and sisters and friends were clinging together, some looking lonely and lost and many decidedly apprehensive. Each child carried a carrier bag or small case containing their night clothes, change of underwear and toothbrush and comb they had been allowed to bring with them and, of course, their gas mask.

'They were mustered in the long corridor and then ushered, a few at a time, in to be examined by the doctor and have their heads searched for lice by the nurse. These operations over, they returned to the corridor where they were sorted out by the Billeting Officer and handed over or delivered to the people with whom they were to stay. It was a horrifying experience, which I shall never forget, to see how some people tried to grab, as quickly as they could, the most cared for and clean looking children; and so sad for the few left at the end and for whom billets had to be found.

'In my home, we had two pairs of brothers and sisters and one of the schoolmasters. I think most of the children settled down reasonably happily though I do remember a knock coming on our door and when my mother opened it, she found a very upset small boy on the doorstep who said, "Please Mrs. Stratton can I be your evacuee?" He had been placed with a very elderly couple who just didn't know how to cope with young children. Tactful arrangements were made and he joined our household.

'Although the children came from a secondary school, it had been arranged that if any had younger brothers or sisters, they should not be separated, so we had to cope with a group not only of secondary pupils but of infants and juniors too. Members of the Flying Bull Lane Staff accompanied their children and had to stay to help with the teaching but none of them were infant teachers. When our classes were finally sorted out and term started, I think I had over fifty five and six year-olds.

'There were now too many children for classrooms, so work time was staggered – some having lessons in the morning and others in the afternoon. Wherever we went, our gas masks came too. Each day started with gas mask drill, so that every child knew exactly what to do should there be a gas attack warning. Fortunately this never happened.

'Large air-raid shelters had already been built on land previously used for allotments further up the Andover Road. We had numerous practices to get out of school and into the shelters quickly. As soon as the warning was given – this was a whistle blown by Mr Wilson – everyone lined up in the playgrounds, where names were checked, then proceeded in orderly crocodile files to the shelters. There was no public siren in the village but if there was a possibility of a raid, the school was warned by telephone and later received the "All clear" the same way.

'To get into the shelters, which were like dark tunnels and smelt damp, one had to go down several steps. The children sat on benches on either side of the shelter. As far as I can remember we lit hurricane lamps to lighten the darkness. At the far end, away from the entrance, a small section was curtained off with some sort of sacking. This compartment was furnished with a bucket and seat as a makeshift toilet. This naturally intrigued the infants and inevitably everyone wanted 'TO GO'! As a teacher, it was hard at times to be firm and say a necessary "No, not yet". While in the shelters, we spent time singing and listening to stories. Usually the Alert was quite short and thankfully we never heard or saw any enemy aircraft during these times.

'For some months the Infants used a large hut at the rear of the Vine Hotel as a supplementary classroom. This entailed taking children up and down the street. Teaching in the Vine Hall was extremely difficult because of the lack of transportable equipment. However, as back in my youth, chanting and singing came into their own and I guess those children knew their tables and phonic sounds better than any have done before or since. Of course, reading books and small items were fairly easy to carry but we had no desks – only the long forms on which the children sat – so writing or drawing of any sort was not easy.'

Mrs Harding shows the difficulties of teaching in wartime, but coping with problems cheerfully and determinedly was the characteristic of most civilians in the war. People who complained about anything were likely to be answered with 'don't you know there's a war on?'.

Laurie Stares recalls that after a time the Flying Bull Lane children went home and others from Gosport came, one of whom lived with his family. New teachers came too and one helped him immensely. The Commercial Wing of Portsmouth Municipal College also arrived, bringing about 100 students aged between 14 and 16. They were billeted around the area and classes were held in Longstock Village Hall, the chapel opposite, Leckford Village Hall and Leckford School. Laurie joined the College in 1941 and his year had 80 girls and 20 boys. As he says, 'a good time was had by all'.

Air Raid Precautions

Keeping an adequate blackout at night was of great importance in making it harder for German bombers to identify towns and villages. One of the first duties of the A.R.P., a voluntary service, was to ensure that the blackout was maintained. Their leading inspector was an ex-policeman, known as 'Put-that-light-out-Fudge' from his way of tapping with his truncheon on windows which had the slightest chink. The A.R.P. also had a responsibility to fight fires, to help at the site of any bombing and, in larger towns, to sound the air-raid sirens which warned of imminent enemy attack and later to notify the 'All Clear'.

The Fire Brigade

At the outset of the war this was still the Stockbridge Volunteer Brigade, under its Captain, Sydney Stares. At first they still used a manual pump but they were then supplied with a Coventry Climax trailer pump which was towed behind Mr Wiltshire's bread van or Mr Stares' Ford 8. The trailer was heavy and on one occasion the bread van was towing it with one fireman, the coalman 'Snowy' Offer, in the back together with a number of foam extinguishers. They were hurrying to a fire in Houghton but at the bend on the hill coming down into Houghton, the trailer took charge and the van turned over, activating some extinguishers: Snowy emerged covered in foam!

Later the brigade became the National Fire Service and received a new motorised tender. All their services were voluntary and their businesses came to a standstill when a call was being answered. This was in keeping with the spirit of the times.

The Home Guard

In the summer of 1940 Germany invaded and overwhelmed its neighbours in Europe from Norway to France. The British Expeditionary Force on mainland Europe was defeated and only just escaped capture through the evacuation from Dunkirk. It seemed very likely that Britain itself would be invaded. As the Army re-grouped it was decided to create a voluntary force which could provide resistance throughout the countryside. Initially called the 'Local Defence Volunteers' this became the 'Home Guard' which was affectionately caricatured in the television series 'Dad's

Army'. Starting without proper weapons or uniform its units trained with wooden dummy rifles or shotguns but they took their responsibilities seriously. A shepherd's hut on Stockbridge Down was manned at night and there were regular drills.

On the lighter side Mick Lunn tells how his father, Alfred Lunn, was the major in charge of the local Home Guard in 1944. As Head Keeper to the Houghton Club he had, on several occasions, taken General Beddell Smith, General Eisenhower's Chief of Staff, fishing on the Test. This was much enjoyed and General Eisenhower also came fishing. Once the invasion of France was well under way the hospitality was returned with an invitation to fly over to France to see how the campaign was progressing. He was told to come in his Home Guard uniform. He had a successful trip, returning with red wine and Camembert and with the tale that he had heard one of our soldiers say to another 'Things must be bad, mate; they've called in the Home Guard.'

The Observer Corps

This was another service manned by volunteers. Its job was to watch the skies, identifying any aircraft which flew over. If any were thought to be enemy planes the authorities would be informed. Aircraft identification was a popular pursuit among the young, many of whom had 'Spotters Clubs' at school. Their opinion was often useful to the adults on watch. At first the stand and hut were situated behind the Grosvenor Hotel but later the post was moved to a site at the top of London Hill, where the view was better.

Road blocks

In anticipation of the possibility of German tanks on English roads, 'blocks' were built on a number of roads, particularly at intersections such as the then crossroads between the London Road, Winton Hill and Somborne Hill. Large concrete blocks at the road edges were accompanied by concrete 'slots' across the roads into which steel spikes could be inserted, if necessary, to create tank barriers. The blocks at the bottom of Somborne Hill, which filled the space between the church and road, were not removed until 1986, so allowing the footpath past the church to be created.

A dummy airfield

Although Stockbridge escaped serious damage from bombs, this was not true of Middle Wallop airfield. A raid there caused considerable damage and several deaths. This was probably the reason why a decision was made to build a mock airfield which had lighted 'runways' and imitation planes. It was spread out over a large part of Houghton Down Farm and North Houghton, the area to the south of the A30 and to the west of the town. Two aircraftsmen and a corporal staffed it, moving the 'planes' around and altering the pattern of lights. Luckily for Stockbridge, although some bombs were dropped on it, none caused any damage to the town.

Spitfire assembly

When the Supermarine factory in Southampton was bombed a decision was made to move the assembly of the famous Spitfire fighter to the road above Chattis Hill Stables, opposite Broughton Road off the A30 to Salisbury. They were put together in huts just off this road and flown out from a runway which had been the gallops for the stables. This has given the road its present name, Spitfire Lane.

Chilbolton Airfield

In 1940 238 Squadron of Hurricanes flew from the airfield established on Chilbolton Down to take part in the Battle of Britain. Numerous other squadrons followed. In 1943 the airfield was rebuilt and in December it was taken over by American Air Force fighter-bomber squadrons. By mid -1944 the airfield was also used as a base to receive casualties flown in Dakotas from the battlefields of Europe. The 33rd Medical Battalion and 1st Platoon of the 6th Field Hospital were joined by the 188th Medical Service and its Ambulance Detachment. The Field Hospital was designated an Air Evacuation Holding Unit supplying stretcher bearers and evacuating battle casualties who would be sent to one of several hospitals in the region, nearly all via the 34th General Hospital at Stockbridge. Full records are not available for the period from D-Day, June 6 1944, but from the end of November 1944 to 1 March 1945, the total number of casualties arriving at Chilbolton Airfield was 21,573. Local residents became used to ambulances rushing through the lanes on their way to and from Stockbridge.

Hospitals in Stockbridge

Another little-known aspect of the way in which the war affected Stockbridge was the large military hospital near the town. This was the US 34th General Hospital which was sited opposite Stockbridge Down and to the east of Somborne Park Road, which leads down to Little Somborne. It was a very substantial unit: with ward blocks, operating theatres, administrative offices and staff quarters, there were about 50 buildings. In addition to the airborne casualties, wounded personnel were also brought to Stockbridge by rail and this continued after the use of the airfield had ceased in March 1945. After their essential treatment many patients were moved by rail to Tidworth Military Hospital or to other hospitals in the Midlands.

After the war the site was used as a holding camp for Polish ex-servicemen and their families. The Andover Advertiser of December 1946 records that ladies from Stockbridge and King's Somborne were giving English lessons to some of the 400 inmates at the Polish Dependants Camp. Next, in 1947, the Royal Army Pay Corps took over the buildings but finally the site was abandoned in 1962.

Another establishment with a wartime medical function was Marsh Court. In the first World War it was used as a convalescent home. Springfield, now Cannon House in London Road, was called 'Marsh Court Hospital 2'. In the second World War it was used by British War Relief for children who had been injured in some way. It was also used as an R.A.S.C. butchery depot (LS).

Dances in the Town Hall. Even in a war there may be time for fun. One local source of enjoyment was the Saturday evening dance in the Town Hall, attended by servicemen from all round the area and by the girls of the town and surrounding villages. One Saturday in 1942 the usual band was unable to come because of heavy snow. Mick Lunn, then 16 and known to play the piano well, was asked by his father if he could 'do something'. He enlisted the help of four friends who played other instruments and they played foxtrots, quicksteps, waltzes and all the usual range of dances. The evening went so well that they were asked to do it again and they formed themselves into the 'Dots and Dashes', so called from the Morse code they had been learning in the Air Training Corps. Before long they were playing up to six nights a week at local dances at Andover, Romsey and many village halls. The group had to disband when Mick reached call-up age in 1944.

Sources

Harding, Monica. (1997) *Remembering Stockbridge and the Primary School from 1920 to 1960*. MPC Publishing, Salisbury.

Lockyer, Eleanor M. (1997) *English Airfield – Chilbolton Memories 1941 – 1945*. Holmes and Son, Andover.

Personal communications from Mick Lunn, Derek Tempero and Laurie Stares.

STOCKBRIDGE SINCE THE WAR

Gain and Loss – Changes in Modern Stockbridge

...mains water and drainage did not reach the town till the 1960s. Many homes still got their water from the river...even emptied their chamber pots into it.

The town to which surviving ex-servicemen returned after the war ended was little different from the one they had left and in the first ten or fifteen years, change came slowly. Because of the economic condition of the country, rationing of food and clothing continued for almost ten years, gradually reducing in its extent. The social structure of the town when Dr Michael Johnson came to practise here in 1951 was one which he describes as 'nobs and villagers'. In other words there were some very wealthy people – at one stage he had four millionaires[30] in his practice – but most of the townsfolk were relatively poor, with no car or telephone. Even possessions like watches were uncommon.

Families were often large and many houses and cottages were small, crowded and insanitary. Side roads such as Blandford Row and New Street were little better than dirt roads. A mains water and drainage system did not reach the town until the 1960s. Till then many homes still got their water from the river and some even emptied their chamber pots into it. There were old cottages where Rosalind Hill House now stands and the small gap in the low wall below the rails was to enable the cottagers to dip, or empty, a bucket, *(fig 22)*. There was also a hand-pump behind where the telephone boxes now stand. This had to be 'primed' with water from the river before it would operate.

The telegraph poles in the High Street with their numerous crossbars, *(fig 20)* giving rise to the joking term 'Dodge City', had not yet been replaced by underground cables. The telephone exchange was still a manual one, the exchange was 'Stockbridge' and the numbers were three figures only. Later the exchange was automated so that the numbers became part of the Andover (now 01264) series, with the prefixes '810' and later '811'. Most of the shops were much the same as in the pre-war period and there were still four petrol filling stations. In 1968 E. C. Fenning at the Grosvenor Garage was advertising a Morris 1300 Traveller at £769.19.0d., so you could even buy a car in Stockbridge.

The changes which have taken place since then, mainly from the 1960s

[30] Remembering that the pound in 1950 was worth nearly 20 of today's pounds.

22 This bend in a carrier stream is popular at weekends with families feeding the ducks and trout. To the right is Rosalind Hill House, on the site of earlier cottages. The small break in the low wall on the right was to allow the residents of the cottages to dip in the river for their water, (or sometimes to empty their chamber pots).

onwards, have reflected what has happened throughout the nation. Television aerials and, later, satellite dishes have appeared. Prosperity has gradually increased so that most families now have at least one car. As car ownership has grown, railway branch lines have closed. There are still buses through the town, run by the Stagecoach company, but there used to be two bus stations. The King Alfred's bus company was on the site of the Hair and Body Barn and the Wilts and Dorset in part of the site now occupied by Waterlow. Both had buses overnight, ready for an early start.

Supermarkets have become widespread and offer a wide range of food and drink at prices which have meant that many village shops have become uneconomic. As a result post offices have also shut down and smaller country towns and villages, which once were virtually self-sufficient, are now dependent on larger towns, often some distance away.

The village pub is no longer the habitual evening haunt of the working man, who now tends to stay home to watch a favourite television programme, perhaps drinking canned beer. This trend has been accentuated by drink-driving laws. Today country pubs are closing every week. Those which remain only prosper if they offer good food. Their customers at lunch-time are mostly the affluent elderly or businessmen and women who have met to enjoy a meal in a pleasant setting. These are some of the ways in which village life in England has changed in the past 50 years. Why then, have these trends not denuded Stockbridge of its shops when other communities with far larger populations have lost theirs?

The Stockbridge paradox

One answer to this question is that the agent which has been responsible for most of the changes outlined above, the motor car, has kept the shops and businesses of Stockbridge alive. It is an attractive town with relatively easy parking[31] and is accessible via a number of main roads, all busy but none of them unduly so: this means that there is a regular 'passing trade'. It lies in a prosperous region and is surrounded by potential customers for 'up-market' shops. Indeed it is not too fanciful to describe the town as an up-market open-air shopping mall. In some cases the presence of several shops of similar type makes it worthwhile for the shopper to visit the town when looking for a particular item.

Another part of the answer is that the town has changed to meet altered circumstances. There are no longer any cobblers in the town, nor a saddler, nor a draper. There is only one butcher, one baker, one filling station and only one dedicated newsagent, though there are two substantial convenience stores. Instead there are a number of antique shops and shops selling crafts and decorative items. There are two art galleries and two shops selling clothing and equipment for country sports. Some pubs have closed but those which remain all offer accommodation and there are eight places in which to get a meal. The result of all these developments is the present distribution of enterprises in the High Street detailed in Chapter 6.

Most of these changes have been gradual but over the years the character of the High Street has altered radically. The biggest changes have been the closure of the railway and the consequent alterations in the road system and new housing developments. The road changes are discussed later. The changes in housing and in social structure are discussed first.

---

[31] A growing problem is the number of cars parked all day because their owners work in one of the shops or other businesses. Most people who work in Stockbridge live elsewhere.

Changes in Housing and Population Trends

The state of many houses and cottages was deeply unsatisfactory after the war. Not only were standards and expectations rising but there had been little maintenance of most properties for the whole of the war period. After the war building materials remained in short supply. The worst affected included the houses built by Barham in the late 18th and early 19th century, but even council houses erected in the pre-war years needed improvement. For example, the first houses in the Roman Road estate, nos 1-14, built in 1935, had no electricity, plumbing or toilets. They shared three outside standpipes and residents had to hand-pump their water into buckets or other containers, heating the water in 'coppers' over coal fires. Toilet facilities were buckets in sheds in the gardens. Not until after the war were flush toilets and boilers introduced and the houses wired. Much the same was true of South Side Cottages.

All this was part of a trend to higher standards which benefited many homes. Yet as those standards rose they contributed to a reduction in the number of people living in the town. This was because in Stockbridge many of the older cottages were demolished and replaced by larger homes, with an overall loss of housing numbers. Even when older premises were not destroyed, some were amalgamated, two houses blending into one.

Another factor reducing the town's population has been that few of the new shop owners have wished to live 'over the shop'. This has left an appreciable amount of accommodation empty: this affects about 15 properties in the High Street (LS). There has been a general reduction in the size of families. At present 34 houses in the High Street are occupied by single people (LS). Finally many of those moving into the town more recently have been retired people with no children at home.

There have, of course, been some new housing developments. The most substantial were those in Trafalgar Way and Nelson Close, built in the mid-1970s and the New Street development, including the surgery, which came some 10 years later. Their prices put these homes out of reach of the young people who had grown up in the town and most have been bought by middle class families. This, together with the loss of many smaller cottages, has totally changed the social structure of the town, which is now predominantly middle class. The reduction in numbers has been a concern to the Parish Council, who have resisted, not always successfully, applications to use existing houses for offices or other types of commercial use. At the time of writing the Test Valley Borough Council is considering a further development in a field between Marsh Court Road and the Test Way just south of Trafalgar Way. This may add some 30 houses, among which there could be starter homes for young couples.

Changes in the Roads[32]

The last to cross the bridge was Brindle, a dog from the White Hart ..though blind it went daily to John Robinson's for a bone… it tried to cross as usual but fell in…it reached the shop for its bone but died under the archway at the side of the shop.

Stockbridge has always lived by its roads. Two east-west roads meet at the eastern end of the town – the A30 from Sutton Scotney and the B3049 (once the A272) from Winchester. As they meet they cross the north-south road, the A3057, which links Romsey and Andover. Outside the town these roads have changed little since the war but there have been significant alterations within the town. The first change followed the final closure of the railway in 1969. This released land which made possible the new roundabouts and linking roads which allow the various traffic streams to merge safely. These changes were completed by 1972. The rearrangement greatly reduced the traffic on London Road, which is a narrow road. It is also a place where some children at the Primary School are entering and leaving the school. Figures 25 and 27 show the layouts before and after these changes.

The demolition of the railway bridge was one of the major events in the town. The last creature to cross the bridge was Brindle, a dog belonging to the White Hart. Although the dog was blind and deaf he went each day to John Robinson's shop for a bone and then returned home. When the roadway had been half-demolished he tried to cross as usual but fell into the gap. He managed to get through for his bone. However the shock was too much and he died under the archway at the side of the shop.

Until the 1960s the A30 was one of the main roads leading to the West Country. It ran south-west from Basingstoke as the A30(T), the 'T' meaning that it was a trunk road. Just after crossing the railway line from Basingstoke to Winchester, it divided, with the A303(T) running west to Andover, while the A30 continued a more southerly route via Sutton Scotney and

[32] Dates kindly provided by the County Surveyor, Hampshire County Council.

23 Looking eastward towards Winton Hill and lower end of London Road in 2000. The low white building was the coach house and stable of the Queen's Head, to which the Ship Inn was previously a neighbour. Today it is Stockbridge Antiques. The White Hart is on the right.

Stockbridge to Salisbury. Though the A30 was 'de-trunked' in 1958, it was still much used. Drivers to the West Country could choose between the A303, with the risks of congestion at the level-crossing in Andover and the A30 through Stockbridge which was less congested but had two humped bridges. At weekends in summer the traffic in the town could be almost at a standstill. Two petrol stations, one at Stokes' Garage, the other at Fennings, now 'Stockbridge Racing' were manned all night.

In 1965 Andover was bypassed and by the early 1980s the A303 had become a dual carriageway as far as the Hampshire-Wiltshire border. This diminished the use of the A30 as a route for traffic to the West Country but it remains a busy road. To the west of Stockbridge it carries traffic to the Wallops and to Salisbury. The road follows a curve as it ascends the hill. The carriageway here was divided in the 1960s, partly to reduce the congestion caused by slow lorries climbing the hill and partly to enable traffic from Test Valley School and Roman Road to enter the A30 more safely.

Changes in the Environment

The last feature to be mentioned in discussing the changes since the war is the environment. It is generally recognised that Britain's environment has suffered in many ways since the Second World War. Housing estates, motorways, quarrying and other developments have reduced the areas of true countryside. Wild flowers have disappeared from many meadows. Hedgerows have been removed or have been neglected so that they become 'gappy' or are invaded by unwanted species such as old man's beard or elder. Birds which once were common have shown a marked decline. As Laurie Stares recalls, 'once on our Common Marsh lapwing nested in profusion, as did skylarks: redshank and snipe would rise from the stream in large numbers.' One reason for their disappearance, as he indicates, is the number of people exercising their dogs on the Marsh; this has driven away ground-nesting birds.

There are, however, many other causes of harm to the environment. Laurie points out that in the twenties and thirties thousands of Hampshire downland acres were left uncultivated due to the depression in farming. The war brought a need to cultivate as much land as possible and this drive has continued to the present day, only slightly modified by the 'set-aside' of some farming land. Better crop husbandry and improved seed quality have meant that whereas in 1940 an acre of the best land would yield a ton of wheat, today even marginal land can approach five tons per acre. Ground which would once have been rough pasture is now cultivated and this has involved some use of pesticides, further reducing the insect species on which birds might feed. The practice of planting wheat in the autumn rather than the spring has cut the number of stubble fields which could feed seed-eating birds through the winter, though the associated autumn ploughing can give a brief feast to rooks, jackdaws and seagulls. Removal of hedgerows has deprived birds and other wildlife of a habitat and a safe route along which to move, unseen by predators.

This is the broad picture of the environment in Britain and Stockbridge has been affected by many of these changes. There are, however, some mitigating features. Nearly all of the Test Valley[33] is an 'Environmentally Sensitive Area' (ESA) which means that farmers can agree to restrict their activities in return for certain payments; however, not all farmers in the valley have agreed to these restrictions. A stronger level of protection is provided by designation as a 'Site of Special Scientific Interest' (SSSI) which controls a landowner's freedom of action though not, currently, his or her

[33] Details kindly provided by the Environment Department, Hampshire County Council.

24 Panoramic view of Stockbridge from the east, taken from the hillside south of Winton Hill. The shadows indicate that it is midday. The church spire, built in 1887, looks new, so the picture probably dates from the 1890s or very early 1900s. The station building is in the lower right hand quadrant with a long barn roof behind it, both since demolished *(courtesy of Jill Harding)*

25 Road system before the closure of the railway and demolition of the bridge and station. All traffic on the A30 went through the London Road. The rectangle beside the railway is the site of the Little Dean football ground *(reproduced by Kenneth Bramer from the Ordnance Survey map with the permission of Her Majesty's Stationery Office, © Crown Copyright, NC/00/1266)*

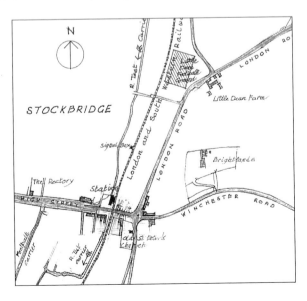

26 Stockbridge in the 1990s, our cover photograph. This view is similar to figure 24 but is taken in morning light and from a point slightly further south. The town has more trees than a century before *(courtesy of Dick Pugh)*. Available as a postcard from Broughton Crafts.

27 Road system today. The site of the new football pitch is shown to the north of the High Street *(reproduced by Kenneth Bramer from the Ordnance Survey map with the permission of Her Majesty's Stationery Office, © Crown Copyright, NC/00/1266)*

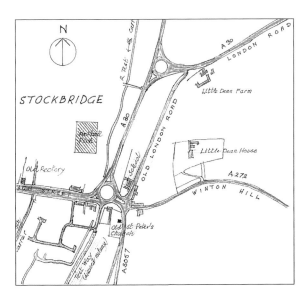

neglect of the land concerned. The whole of the River Test is an SSSI and above and below Stockbridge there are other designated sites, notably the Common Marsh and Stockbridge Down. In addition, the private nature of the fishing areas and some estates reduces human and canine disturbance and this creates havens for wildlife which may then be seen elsewhere. As well as the common bird life widely seen from roads and footpaths, swans, geese, mallard, coot, moorhens, rooks, seagulls and the ubiquitous pheasants, less common birds may be seen. These include buzzards, herons, an occasional red kite (recently reintroduced), a few skylarks or a barn owl floating across the beam of the car headlights. From time to time egrets or a cormorant may be seen. Away from areas disturbed by humans, other species, such as Cetti's warbler, are to be found. In gardens, birds such as robins, wrens, tits, finches, blackbirds and pigeons are still common, with green and spotted woodpeckers as occasional visitors.

In the fields rabbits abound again but hares are less common. Foxes and hedgehogs are seen or leave their droppings. Fallow and muntjac deer are spotted from time to time. Otters have not yet reappeared on the Test but water-voles are re-establishing themselves now that mink are being trapped.

The Millennium has been celebrated in Stockbridge by the very welcome planting of trees but this does not mean that the town lacks trees. Our cover picture shows how green the town is. Even the two 'new' roundabouts, now more than a quarter of a century old, have become small copses.

Our environment shows many losses over the past fifty years but by present day standards it is holding its own and Hampshire remains a beautiful county in which to live. The greatest threats all come from human activity. This is why the areas from which the public are excluded, such as the river banks and the large estates, are often de facto nature reserves. Those who are irritated because they cannot go to such sites should remember that their absence may enable species under pressure to survive!

It is encouraging that the pupils from the Test Valley School put the wild life areas as one of the features they would hope to see preserved (see Chapter 12). It will be their generation which has to make sure that this happens.

6 The High Street

Visitors to Stockbridge may want to shop, to eat or to browse in a gallery, gift shop or antique shop. They may just want to wander, looking in windows and at interesting buildings. This picture of the High Street in this millennial year includes the latter.

The town of Stockbridge ends at the bridge over the River Test and all to the west of the river is Longstock. Since this distinction is not important to the visitor the tour begins on the Salisbury Hill.

Test Valley School, built in 1961 as a mixed comprehensive school, now takes 600 pupils aged between 11 and 16. There are 39 teachers and 17 non-teaching staff working with the Headteacher, Miss Wendy Morrish. Pupils come mainly from a large catchment in the Test Valley, between Andover and Romsey. The facilities include classrooms, laboratories, workshops, drama and music facilities, information technology area and library. There are also a gymnasium, tennis courts, playing fields and a large open-air swimming pool.

The Hair and Body Barn opened in 1998 when this listed barn, whose outer structure had been restored, was refitted internally to provide attractive modern facilities in which a range of services are available to both sexes including all forms of hairdressing, beauty treatments and aromatherapy, carried out by a team of professional stylists and therapists.

In the lower Longstock Road:

Hawksdown Veterinary Centre is based in Windover Farm and is a branch of the Hawksdown Veterinary Centre in Winchester. It is staffed by Mr J.M. and Mrs C.N. Donnell and two veterinary nurses. It opened as 'Tutt and Sons' in 1988 and the present owners took over in 1996. It offers a local service for Stockbridge and surrounding villages, opening for two to three hours five days a week.

The Corn Loft Art Studio is a small painting and pottery studio in what used to be a corn store in Windover Farm. It provides leisure and educational opportunities for local adults and children, with therapeutic programmes for children and adults with special physical, educational or emotional needs. Jeff Walker is Arts Tutor and Dr Alexander (Sandy) Burnfield supervises his therapeutic work.

Windover Farm is part of Burnfield Farms, a family partnership with five members. It is the home of Chris and Jane Reynell, Jane being one of the Burnfield family. Chris Reynell has invented a new system for treating household waste, including newspapers, and garden waste or farm materials such as manure and slurry. They are broken down by 'anaerobic digestion' using bacteria which thrive in the absence of oxygen. Competing commercial systems all have drawbacks. The Reynell method, for which there are patents (under the name Bioplex), is faster than others and can work on a small or large scale. For farm waste it is possible to use temperatures high enough to kill dangerous bacteria. The end-products are compost-like or manure-like substances, depending on the original material. Another by-product is the gas methane, which can be used to generate electricity. It is hoped that farm-scale trials will soon be evaluated at Sparsholt College and Reading University.

And in the Houghton Road:

The Carbery Guest House lies on the corner of Salisbury Hill and Houghton Road. With 11 bedrooms it caters for a wide clientele from the UK and overseas. Ann and Philip Hooper bought it in 1965. Among many other improvements, the range of flint walls around and behind the house were built by Philip Hooper himself, a huge undertaking which involved the removal of 400 loads of soil. The house is Georgian and was earlier called Clarendon House.

The Cossack is now a private house but was a pub until 1966. It was named after a Derby winner trained by the Day family – local trainers in the 19th century. Originally the next-door building, now the house called **Papillon,** was part of the inn and contained the landlord's sitting room and the stables. Its present front wall was once occupied by stable doors and in the 18th and 19th centuries cart-horses were kept there, ready to hire out to help to pull heavy carriages, such as the London to Exeter coach, up Salisbury Hill – these were the so-called 'cock-horses' or 'trace-horses'.

Drover's House *(fig 6)* is one of the best known houses in the area because of the Old Welsh writing on its wall, which means 'seasoned hay, rich grass, good ale, comfortable rest'. Chapter 3 describes the droving of cattle and sheep but the house is much older than the droving trade, with parts believed to date from the 12th century when it was owned by the Bishop of Winchester.

Hermit Lodge was at one stage Hermit Cottage before being enlarged. Its name comes not from the Derby winner of 1867, but from an earlier horse called Hermit owned by John Day. This horse was buried across the road in what is now the garden of Medlar Cottage when it was the kitchen garden to Hermit Lodge. During race meetings Edward, Prince of Wales, stayed here while Lillie Langtry stayed across the river. Lily Cottage next door was once part of Hermit Lodge: the footbridge from its garden leads to the garden of the White House. It is said to have been built at the Prince's request after an earlier bridge had collapsed under his weight (GM).

Across the bridge over the Test and into the High Street (North Side)

Clarendon House contains three enterprises. **Aspect International Telecoms** under Bob Keating provide telecommunication services of all types from provision of mobile phones to installation of telecom facilities in business premises. **Robert Walster Associates** are civil engineers. **Dr Nick Badham** is a consulting minerals exploration geologist.

Brockmans is a solicitors' practice which was founded in October 1992 with a view to providing highly professional advice from approachable people at reasonable cost. The practice has grown steadily and now represents clients, both private and corporate, locally, in London, in the provinces and internationally. There are currently seven solicitors and a full support staff and further growth is anticipated.

The Greyhound, licensee Peter Harding, dates from the 15th Century and is one of the survivors of Stockbridge's thirteen inns of a century ago. It has the 'Les Routiers' award for its food. It provides accommodation and, among other services, it offers access to fishing on local lakes and river beats.

George Hofman Antiques 'At the sign of the Black Cat' has been selling antiques on this site for many years. He now concentrates on restoration work. In his former premises are:

> **Jane Baigent** A shop specialising in painted furniture, plain and embroidered linen and decorative items.

The Owl and the Pussycat A gift shop, run by Suzannah Jackson, almost entirely sourced from British suppliers, selling hand-painted silk scarves, silk flowers, cushions, cards and many other items.

Lloyds TSB began as Lloyds Bank in Stockbridge in 1919, when it was on the site now occupied by the Co-op, in the front room of the home of Frank Wiltshire, whose bakery was next door, *(fig 20)*. It moved to the present premises after the war. It now serves personal customers and the local businesses. Most customers are known by name, an unusual and welcome feature in a bank today.

Stockbridge Pharmacy has been run by Michael and Mary Tuff since 1987 but was already a pharmacy. It provides a service to Stockbridge and surrounding villages, making up NHS prescriptions and selling a wide range of proprietary products. In addition, like many pharmacies, it gives advice on the management of basic ailments, which reduces the load on GPs.

Robjents was started in 1998 by Alistair Robjent. He specialises in country clothing and in equipment for shooting enthusiasts and fly fishermen. The shopper will find 'London quality goods at country prices'. There is also a gallery of wildlife paintings by the owner's father, Richard Robjent.

Stokes' Garage *(fig 28)* is one of the most distinctive features of the High Street with its colourful exterior, its balcony and with the 'dial' petrol pumps in front of it. 'Stockbridge House', as it is called, was built in the later years of the 19th century by Mr Brock. His daughter, son-in-law and family lived there. The balcony is thought to have been intended to allow the owners and their guests to watch the parades of carriages, coaches and nobility in the High Street in the time of the Danebury races[34]. It was started as a bicycle repair shop and garage by Mr Thomas Parker in 1919. In 1964 Mr John Stokes took it over, continuing this tradition. The range of hardware on sale is remarkable: anyone who lacks, for example, a nut or a washer, a nail or a light bulb should start at Stokes'.

Baptist Chapel (Steadman Memorial Church) is the latest chapel on this site. In the 19th century there was a cottage by the roadside, in front of an earlier chapel. The present chapel was built in 1905 in front of a mission hall, later replaced by a meeting room. A drop in the level of the stream alongside the chapel has affected the brickwork and an extensive

[34] There are unconfirmed but widespread tales that the balcony once served to display the charms of some ladies of easy virtue to the visitors to the town, especially those on their way to the races.

28 Stokes' Garage, one of the most unusual buildings in the High Street. The design is thought to have been inspired by a visit to Italy. The petrol pumps are still of the old 'dial' type, measuring gallons.

programme of repairs is being undertaken. The Lay Pastor, Mr Trevor Timewell, comes from Southampton for a weekly service at 10.30 am on Sundays, with a monthly 6.00 pm Sunday service. He visits parishioners at least once a week. In addition there is an interdenominational women's meeting each Thursday. From time to time concerts are held in this building.

The Sheriff's House, as its name suggests, was once the equivalent of today's police station. Although it is now the home of Ernest and Joan Fisher, the old door to the cells still remains inside.

The Stockbridge Peking A Chinese restaurant and 'take-away' is an unexpected find in a small country town but Choi's Restaurant came to the High Street in 1989 and became the Stockbridge Peking in 1992. Clients come from all over the neighbourhood to enjoy the Pekinese, Cantonese and seafood cuisine. There is also a take-away service which includes some Indian dishes.

St Peter's Church *(fig 29)* This Victorian Gothic style Parish Church was built in 1866 when Old St Peter's became unfit for worship due to dampness. The tower and spire were added in 1887. To save money the people of Stockbridge used barrows to move a number of items, including the bells, a 12th century stone crucifix, 13th century font and other stonework from the old church to the new one. In 1990 the church was severely affected

29 St Peter's Church. It was built in 1866 to replace Old St Peter's. At first it had only a small tower. In 1887 the full tower and spire were added above the stone line.

by damp, rotting floors and a blocked stormwater drainage system. A major programme of restoration was needed, costing £73,000. By 1994 the church had been restored to health. Two millennial projects have also been completed. One was the restoration of the west window and porch window. The other has been the installation of floodlighting, which gives a pleasantly mellow glow to the church at night.

30 The Grosvenor Hotel, another characteristic feature of the High Street. The semicircular room above the pillars is the club room of the Houghton Fishing Club.

The Grosvenor Hotel *(fig 30)* was founded in about 1790 on the site of the King's Head Inn. It was later extended to include adjacent buildings, including the former Market Room. The pillared portico has graced the High Street for some two centuries, during which the name has been variously the Grosvenor Arms Hotel, the Red Lion Hotel and the Commercial Hotel. The Houghton Fishing Club now owns the hotel, which is managed by Greene King Inns and Hotels. The club's meeting room is located over the portico. There are various dining and function rooms as well as 21 bedrooms.

The Frame Shop was started in 1989 by Jo Sunter and, as its name implies, it provides all types of framing. A large number of framed prints mainly of dogs and of country sports, such as hunting, shooting and fishing, are on display.

The Co-op underwent extensive renovation and enlargement in 1999 and is now a large self-service store selling many types of food, household products, alcoholic and other beverages. It is open daily from 7.0 am to 11.0 pm.

31 The eastern end of the High Street in April 2000 showing a sign warning of its coming closure for the millennial Passion Play. The grey-white building is Old Swan House and to its left is King's Head House. Once they were a single building, the Swan Inn. After their division in 1869 the eastern half was modified so that its facade resembles stone. The ornate chimney suggests that the building was originally Elizabethan.

King's Head House and Old Swan House *(fig 31)* Until 1869 these two properties together formed the Swan Inn. Then the building was sold in two halves. The name King's Head House might suggest that it was once the King's Head Inn, but this name is relatively recent. It may refer to the fact that in 1688 King James II dined in the Swan Inn on his way to encounter the newly landed William of Orange. The Swan Inn was a coaching inn, providing accommodation, refreshments and fresh horses to travellers[35]. The difference in appearance of the two ends of what was once a single building is the result of a major alteration during the Victorian period when the eastern end was modified to fit the current fashions. The bricks were faced with stucco to simulate stone pillars and stone window lintels while the windows were reduced in size.

[35] The Winchester Newspaper of July 18 1791 contained the following advertisement: 'SWAN INN, STOCKBRIDGE. Thomas Winter, late butler to George Byng, Esq., M.P. begs leave to acquaint the nobility and gentry and his friends in general, that he has taken those extensive and well accustomed premises, the SWAN INN at STOCKBRIDGE, which he has fitted up and improved in such a superior style, as to render it in every point unexceptionable for the reception of families travelling the great Western Road. He has procured a large stock of the choicest WINES; and will exert himself to the utmost in gaining the patronage of the public by his attention and assiduity. Neat POST-CHAISES and ABLE HORSES.'

Lane Antiques occupies part of Old Swan House. This, the eastern part of the property, has, since 1929, been a hardware shop, a labour exchange and a ladies' hairdresser. In 1981 it became an antique shop owned by Mrs Eve Lane, specialising in porcelain, glass, decorative items and small furniture. The splendid chimneys are a notable feature.

The Recreation Ground was opened in 1976. It has a parking area, a pavilion, a football pitch and a children's playground. It is a registered charity, supported by the Stockbridge Parish Council, (who are custodial trustees), Test Valley Borough Council and a number of other bodies.

The Telephone Exchange, lying beside the Recreation Ground access, is a fully digital automated exchange.

Stockbridge Primary School was built in 1910, before which the children were taught in Stockbridge Town Hall. It has since been extended to provide five classrooms, a library, a hall, a staff room, offices and other facilities. In addition to the Headteacher, Simon Francis, there are five teachers and 14 other full-time and part-time staff. In all, some 130 children are divided into two groups, Infants (years 1 and 2) and Juniors (years 3–6). Ages range from 4 to 11 and there are about 25 children in each class.

The Playgroup is located in an external building which is separate from the school. There has been a playgroup in Stockbridge for at least 25 years. For the past ten it has been run by Helen Bryant and six staff members, together with volunteers. There are 50 children on the register with ages from two years and nine months to five years. Up to 24 children come to each of the five morning and three afternoon sessions.

Stockbridge Antiques Centre was originally the coach house of the Queen's Head Inn and was converted to a garage and filling station by Charles Simmonds in 1930. The licence to sell petrol was withdrawn in the mid-1980s. The northern end of the coach house became Queen's Head Cottage and May Cottage while the remainder was used for a variety of commercial purposes. It became an antique shop in the 1990s and the present owner, Tim Baker, took over in January 2000. He specialises in country furniture, mainly antique.

The High Street (South Side)

The White House, once Grosvenor House, was the home in which Lillie Langtry stayed during the race meetings which she attended with Prince

Edward in the 1890s. The house was built for Robert Grosvenor, 1st Marquess of Westminster. A map of 1790 shows that immediately to the west of it there was a toll house and a toll gate before the bridge over the Test.

Folklore was brought to Stockbridge in 1995 by Jenny Percival. It is full of every kind of gift, from teddy bears and other stuffed animals of all sizes to painted furniture, from cards to decorated mirrors. There are items both old and new. The shop claims to have a ghost but this is not for sale.

Chatterbox Flowers opened on this site in September 2000. Fiona Doyle started her business in Admiral's Row, ten years ago. After a period away from Stockbridge she returned to the premises now occupied by Diligence but the present site, which until 1999 was the Caravan Café[36], offered more space for all aspects of her work, both in direct retailing and flowers for functions. She plans to serve tea and coffee once the flower business is fully installed.

The Three Cups, managed by licensees Paul and Lucy Foster, dates from the 15th century. For much of the last century it was used as a builder's premises and home to the Fowgies family, well known in Stockbridge. It resumed as a inn and restaurant with a full licence in 1996. Fish dishes are a speciality. It lies at the lowest point in the High Street and was liable to flooding, hence the low wall outside.

The Public Toilets were upgraded in 1997 and are now of a high standard.

The Post Office and General Stores provides groceries, chilled and frozen food and a very wide range of wines and spirits. It also offers a variety of other products such as stationery. It is open daily from 9 am to 8 pm. The Post Office is, like most sub-post offices, franchised to the store owner, Ronald Coates. Unusually, the local postal delivery and collection services, which are run by the Royal Mail, work from premises connected to the store. Eight postmen deliver to the surrounding area and collect mail from some 40 boxes. These collections then go to Winchester to be sorted.

Broughton Crafts, owned by Dick and Gillian Pugh, began in 1982 in a barn outside Broughton. Their aim was to sell the best of British craftsmanship. The present premises had been an antique shop. However the site, together with the adjacent Post Office, was threatened with development as a convenience store. This project was abandoned because of the requirement for deep pilings in new buildings and so, in 1983,

---

[36] The original 'café' was a caravan on the road outside the site of the present public toilets. It stayed open all night.

Broughton Crafts were able to move in. The shop has been very successful, selling crafts from many parts of the UK – weaving and wood, cards and candles, games and glasses, baskets and bangles. Customers come from all parts of the south of England, especially before Christmas, and goods are sent throughout the world[37].

Orvis is a branch of a well-known American purveyor of equipment for angling and of outdoor clothing. It moved to the site in the 1980s. Its 'trade mark', a stuffed bear, 5 foot high, stands on the pavement outside, with a fishing rod held upright. Inside is an array of rods, reels, lines and flies, with much other fishing equipment and country clothing. Fly fishing tuition and chalkstream letting are available.

St Thomas More Roman Catholic Church lies behind Rosalind Hill House. It has been established on this site probably since the 1920s. Prior to that there was a Congregationalist chapel and then, for a time, the building was used for film and slide shows.

Mass is held every Sunday at 11.0 am and attracts a congregation of about 80 from Stockbridge and the surrounding area. The priests, under Father Kieran Flynn, S.M.M., come from St John the Baptist, Andover. There are also six lay special ministers, both men and women, who assist the priest to give communion and can give communion in homes.

32 Since it was built in 1790 the Town Hall has played a central part in Stockbridge life. Today it needs extensive renovation and alteration to bring it into line with the needs and standards of the 21st century.

The Town Hall *(fig 32)* was built in 1790, financed by Joseph Foster Barham and George Porter. The clock was added in 1794 and electrified for the

[37] As an example of this market, a bagatelle set was ordered from California. The buyer was quite happy to accept that the cost of express mailing exceeded the cost of the game itself.

Jubilee celebrations of 1935. Originally the front was open to form a market area. It was enclosed in 1810, hence the date on the front and on the clock. The hall has been a focus for town activities throughout its life. Today it needs refurbishment and a grant application has been made for funds for a major series of further improvements.

Courcoux & Courcoux gets its name from the husband and wife team who set up the original gallery in Salisbury. It moved to Stockbridge in 1996. The gallery specialises in contemporary sculpture and paintings with some ceramics. The work of established and of up-and-coming artists is on show.

The Wykeham Galleries were opened by Sally Milligan in 1985 with the aim of selling the work of both new and established contemporary artists. There are numerous paintings as well as sculptures in bronze and wood, ceramics and glass engravings. The nine exhibitions which are held each year draw viewers from a wide area of southern England.

Stockbridge Racing was the site of Fenning's Garage, run by Eric Fenning. His son, John Fenning, was once a racing driver. When, in the 1960s, he tried to find safety harnesses for racing cars there were none. Adapting aircraft harnesses designed by Major 'Dumbo' Willans he set about manufacturing them for all types of competitive driving. Today the harnesses, made in Stockbridge, are exported all over the world and are used by three Formula One and two Indy Car teams. Orders for 500-1000 belts are not unusual. If, on close-ups of pit-stops, you see the name Willans on the driver's harness, you will know it comes from Stockbridge.

Police Station The police station replaced an earlier one which fronted onto the street. A sergeant and eight officers comprise the team and their beat covers the area from the A34 to the Anna Valley, east to west, and from the A303 to five miles south of King's Somborne.

Evans & Partridge often has visitors to the town gazing in its windows, perhaps hoping to find a house in the neighbourhood, perhaps simply dreaming. Residential village sales in the area are a major and thriving part of the business but the partnership of Tim Evans and John Partridge also has agricultural interests. In particular, they run specialist auctions of antique and modern shotguns and fishing tackle and of agricultural vintage equipment (steam tractors, stationary engines and farming bygones).

George Clark, founded in 1994, is primarily concerned with interior design, especially furnishings and fabrics. However they also stock a wide variety of other decorative items which could embellish a home, such as paintings, porcelain, glassware, découpage, cushions, lights and baskets, to name but a few.

For Goodness' Sake has been on this site since 1984 and is owned by Anthony Wallace-Turner. He sells the products typical of a delicatessen – caviar, foie gras, smoked trout, hams, terrines, patés and high quality cheeses – with excellent local home-made pies and cakes. He also offers a house party catering service, boardrooms lunches and gift hampers.

Diligence is a studio/showroom which opened in June 2000. Peter Beresford-Stooke imports specialised French wood-burning stoves known in the UK as 'Focus Fires'. Stoves are custom made, usually for architects or interior designers, but private clients are welcome.

At this point in the High Street there is a reminder of the times when horses, or even cattle, were common in the town. By the stream between Lillie and Diligence a concrete ramp leads down to the stream's edge. This is where animals were once brought to the water for a drink.

Lillie of Stockbridge was started in 1992 by Bernard van Galen as a bakery and tearoom, on the site of the Waggon and Horses. He chose a name which spoke of Stockbridge's long fascination with Lillie Langtry. The quality of his bread, croissants and pastries ensured its success. He and Ninya retired in 1998, but today, under Robert Wilson and David Atkinson, the quality is maintained. The early morning aroma of baking is one of the town's

33 Today's equivalent to Wiltshire's is Lillie of Stockbridge, the bakery and tea-rooms.

delights. Queues may even occur at breakfast time. The tearooms too are busy, especially at weekends, with visitors enjoying baguette sandwiches, cakes or pastries.

Gaynor moved to Stockbridge in 1992. This ladies' clothes shop was founded by Gaynor Luckett in Andover and operated there for 14 successful years. The shop offers a relaxed and welcoming atmosphere in which clients can find comprehensive and individual ranges of high quality clothing, both stylish casual wear and beautiful occasion wear complemented by shoes, hats, jewellery and other accessories.

Groves' is the latest newsagents, confectioners and tobacconists' shop on this site. It began before the War as Orpwood's. It later became Whiffen's, then Buckland's and for some 30 years it has been Groves'. This is one of the shops which almost everyone visits week by week, if not daily; a shop where you bump into people. 'Ally' (Alasdair) Cox has managed it since 1990 with friendly calm despite the early hours which are involved. Collecting the newspapers from the wholesalers begins at 4.30 am. At weekends there is the additional labour of putting together 10 or 12 different elements in the massive Saturday and Sunday papers.

Elizabeth Viney comes from a long line of furniture makers and restorers dating from the 18th century. She sells small, rare and unusual pieces of English period furniture, metalware and treen[38] at 'Jacob's House', purchased in 1967 from the Jacob Family, who were well-known local saddlers. Visits may be made after arranging an appointment or by chance.

John Robinson is generally known as 'John Rob's'. It is one of Stockbridge's best known shops *(fig 19)* and is a first class butcher. John Robinson bought Jim Corrall's shop in 1969 and built it up to be a busy, popular enterprise selling very high quality meat, game, home-made sausages and various cooked meats. His sons, Paul, and twins, Peter and Jonathan, took over in 1994 and have continued this success. Paul reached an even wider public by his resistance to the 1998-99 government ban on beef-on-the-bone. Today there are 11 butchers at work on an average day, while at Christmas there may be many more, with queues onto the pavement sometimes as far as Groves'. Outside catering and barbecues are another aspect of this flourishing business.

---

[38] 'Treen' are small items of wood, especially eating and drinking vessels of past times.

Stockbridge Fire Station Stockbridge is unusual in having had its own fire service for about 101 years. It has come a long way since the days of a horse-drawn, man-pumped engine described earlier. The service covers the region roughly between Wherwell and Mottisfont and from Up Somborne to Lopcombe – the largest area covered by one 'pump' station in Hampshire. At present the station is manned by 12 part-time retained firefighters under the leadership of Sub Officer A. Perry. They train every Monday evening. During an average year there are about 120 calls to house fires, road traffic accidents, special service calls and automatic fire alarms.

J and S Sykes In 1973 Jim Inglis started a greengrocer's shop on this site and John and Sue Sykes took over in 1990. They sell a full range of fruit and vegetables and a selection of fresh and smoked fish, together with some flowers.

The Vine, managed by licensee Fred Lundberg, is another of the town's long-standing pubs. Like the others it offers accommodation and is proud of the quality of its food. Fish dishes are a speciality.

Dance's is a haulage firm operating from the lane next to Squirrels. It is so unobtrusive that many Stockbridge residents are not aware of it, still less that it is now run by the third generation of the Dance family. In 1948 Roy Dance moved to the present premises and started a livestock and general haulage business. His brother, Bert, purchased the business in 1959. In 1969 Alan joined his father as a partner. Upon Bert's retirement in 1972 Alan ran the business until his retirement in 1995. Today the business is managed by Trevor Dance, grandson of Bert. Their main work is in transporting grain from local farms to flour mills and maltsters and to the docks for export.

'Squirrels' This building now houses three firms:

> **Jonathan Shirley** Jonathan Shirley and his father Martin sell antique furniture and modern fabrics but a major part of their business is the restoration of furniture, in which Jonathan is an expert. His workshops are at Chilbolton Down.

> **The Bakhtiyar Galley** Upstairs at Squirrels is a changing display of Persian carpets, runners and kelims, coming from the Bakhtiyar London warehouse.

> **Terra Firma Tiles.** Grace and Charles Wilkinson took over the eastern end of the Squirrels building in 1999. Already established in

North London, and with a warehouse in East Grimstead, they have a wide range of terracotta, slate and stone floor tiles and mainly handmade wall tiles, some imported from Italy.

Round the corner in New Street:

The Game Larder Inn and Restaurant is a former malt-house and brewery which was converted into a restaurant in 1981. Terry and Kerry Jayne are proud of the fine old beams and of the varied food and wine on offer; everything from bar meals to major functions.

The Stockbridge Practice opened the New Street Health Centre in 1984/5 and has four main partners: Drs Gareth Evans, Paul Manchett, Adrian Townsend and David Simpson and a practice manager, Mrs Pauline Webster. A registrar in training is attached for a year and there is often a 'retainer', a part-time doctor whose children are still young. Two health visitors, five district nurses, a physiotherapist, a midwife and a phlebotomist are all attached, some of them part-time. A further 14 part-time staff maintain the administrative and clerical aspects of the practice, which is now fully computerised. There is a branch surgery at Broughton and the practice serves 8,000 patients and covers an area of about 110 square miles around Stockbridge. This practice aims to provide a high standard of health care and their work is much appreciated in the district. Described by Monica Harding (resident for 80 years – see her contributions earlier) as 'a wonderful team of nurses and doctors'.

Further still, in Nelson Close:

Wendy Keith Designs works from 'a half converted garage', where Wendy Keith creates designs for bespoke knitwear and sportswear. The designs are then hand knitted in rural workshops all over Britain and are sought by discriminating clients throughout the world, including many royal families in Europe.

At the end of the village, by the roundabout:

The White Hart is an old coaching inn which has recently undergone extensive renovation, and re-opened in late April, 2000. It has a bar, a restaurant and accommodation for up to 30 guests including three rooms with facilities for disabled or infirm guests.

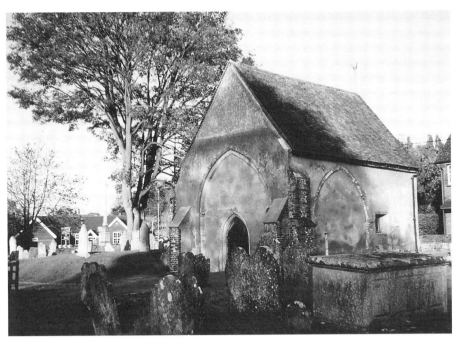

34 Old St Peter's seen from the south-east. This chancel is all that remains of the church shown in Fig 5. In the background to the left are the Lutyens War Memorial and the Primary School.

Old St Peter's Church *(fig 34)* was built on the site of an earlier Saxon chapel. Until 1842 it was a chapel dependent on the 'head-minster' of King's Somborne. By 1863 it was felt to be unfit for use and the new church was built in the High Street. The chancel of the old church survived demolition and was renovated, first in 1963 and more completely in 1990-91. It was re-dedicated and is still in regular use.

On Winton Hill

Little Dean House is a 27-bedded nursing home converted from a substantial 19th century country house.

Stockbridge Riding School and Livery Service, run by John and Phoebe Wrayton, began 30 years ago in the High Street. Since moving to the present site it has grown to accommodate 25 horses. John is also Hayward to the Courts Baron and Leet.

Why are the pavements such a 'patchwork'?

Observant visitors to the High Street will notice that the pavements have a wide variety of surfaces. There is a story behind this odd variation. Today the road is tarmacked but even in the 20th century it has not always been tarred. The Andover Advertiser, in May of 1918, described the 'Dust Peril in Stockbridge'. It reported the complaint that in the dry weather there were major dust clouds from the loose road surface caused by 160 journeys a day undertaken by heavy lorries working from the station and also the traffic of the many light cars employed in military work. It was generally agreed that the road needed tarring but fishing interests stood in the way, fearing that run-off from the tar would affect the fish.

Eventually, at some time in the 1920s, the central part of the roadway was tarred and gravelled but even then the edges, including the areas now used for parking, remained as gravelled strips, as they were owned by the Lord of the Manor and were termed 'manorial wastes'. In 1932 the Lord of the Manor, Sir Norman Hill, agreed that the County Council should make up and maintain the majority of these strips, though the road edges remained gravelled until after the War. Photographs from the early 1930s show there were still no pavements, see figure 20. Most of what is now the pavement remained in the ownership of the Manor. When, in 1946, the areas owned by the Lord of the Manor were transferred to the National Trust, they registered these strips of pavement as 'common land'.

This meant that there were places where most of the pavement was owned by the Trust with other parts owned by the Hampshire County Council. Quite often the surfacing of the pavement was left to the owners of the various properties. The result has been an interesting patchwork, sometimes with a different surface on the house side of the pavement from the road side. Many householders used the 'setts' from the stables which used to be situated behind shops and pubs. Most were the diamond latticed Staffordshire Blue setts but you can find a number of other patterns.

Until 2000, therefore, parts of the pavements were owned by the National Trust but they did not have the staff or experience to maintain them. The surfaces became increasingly uneven and in recent years a number of visitors have tripped and fallen. In January, after prolonged and determined pressure by David Baseley, chairman of the Stockbridge Parish Council, an agreement was reached to upgrade the faulty areas.

This upgrading took place between May and July. The pavements are now even but there are still a variety of different surfaces often on the two sides of the same pavement. From now on the County Council has responsibility for the whole of the footway.

Behind the shops and houses

Another odd feature of the High Street is hidden from view. The map in figure 35 shows the surprising arrangement of the garden plots on the north side. Most of the gardens are hardly wider than the house to which

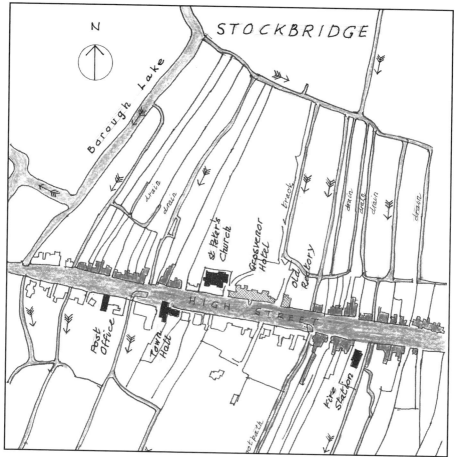

35 Map showing the system of streams and garden plots which still exist on the north side of the High Street. The 'Borough Lake' is the name given to this part of the Test just above Stockbridge. This map shows five streams running under the High Street. With the main channel to the west and a further channel at the eastern end, a total of seven streams pass under the road *(reproduced by Kenneth Bramer from the Ordnance Survey map with the permission of Her Majesty's Stationery Office, © Crown Copyright, NC/00/1266)*

they belong, but some extend back between 100 and 150 metres (340 – 500 feet). If you visit one of these gardens in the Open Gardens weekend in August you will find that they grow steadily marshier and more beset with reeds the further north you go. There are numerous carrier streams and drains among the gardens. It is likely that these and the narrow garden strips date from the 'burgage plots' of the mediæval period, which were discussed earlier. There were once similar plots on the south of the High Street. The evidence has largely disappeared today, but when the Trafalgar Way and Nelson Close developments took place it was necessary for all the owners of the land to agree jointly to sell their 'strips'.

7 Behind the Scenes in Stockbridge

In addition to the enterprises listed in the High Street, there are many activities whose life extends beyond the buildings in which they are based. Since the total is too large for a full description, a number are simply listed in the Appendix. Those described here are some of the major players in the life of the town.

Parish Council – Chairman, David Baseley

'Your Parish Council never lets go.' Borough Council official.

The Parish Council is the most local part of the system of local government. It meets in the Town Hall every month except in August and holds an Annual Meeting, open to the public, each April. It has nine members, in addition to the Clerk and Chairman. They are elected every four years.

It deals with day-to-day matters, such as complaints about street cleaning and litter, overflowing street drains, faulty street lights or overgrown trees. The state of the path to the Common Marsh has been discussed many times. There is hardly a section of the pavement or a street light in the High Street which has not been the subject of a discussion nor a bollard whose siting is not the outcome of careful thought. Study of the minutes shows how long it may take for action to be achieved even when the Parish Council is clear on what needs to be done. Letters are sent to the County or Borough Council, site inspections are made, the councils concerned plead lack of funds and further pressures or negotiations follow. Success is nearly always due to unremitting persistence, as in the example of the upgrading of the High Street pavements, which was mentioned in the last chapter. On one occasion a grudging compliment was given by a council official 'Your Parish Council never lets go'.

There was, for example, a long campaign to create a lay-by opposite to the drive leading to the cemetery on Winton Hill. This was needed to allow funeral parties to make a U-turn into or out of the sharply angled drive on the other side of the road. It took well over a decade to negotiate and implement this necessary change. Similarly, when the road improvements following the closure of the railways took away the football ground, planning permission for the new site was granted in 1972 but conveyance of the land was completed in 1976 and the council was still discussing the funding of its facilities in 1977.

The final element in its work is to comment on all planning applications so that local opinion is available to the planning authority. For the most part these are not contentious but some applications are opposed. In 1991 permission was sought to create a landfill site on Houghton Down to the north of the A30. This led to a vigorous public campaign under the heading 'STOPPIT' which eventually succeeded in blocking the proposal, mainly on the grounds of the likely contamination of water in the river.

The Churches – St Peter's Parish Church and Old St Peter's Church by John Stephenson, Churchwarden

The churches are part of the United Benefice of Stockbridge and Longstock and Leckford. The latter two churches are independent but share the services of the incumbent who is Rector of St Peter's, Stockbridge, and of St Nicholas', Leckford, and Vicar of St Mary's, Longstock. The Reverend Peter Aves resigned in October 2000 after seven years and a successor has yet to be appointed. All three churches have their own churchwardens, secretary and treasurer. St Peter's and St Mary's have separate Parochial Church Councils.

There are 124 members on the electoral roll of St Peter's. Congregations for the early morning communion services at Old St Peter's are about 20, while there are 60 – 70 at the average congregation at St Peter's, rising to 200 at Easter, Christmas and Harvest Festival. A flourishing Sunday School meets twice a month.

The church in Stockbridge is proud of a number of aspects of its life. First is the friendly, welcoming and supportive feeling which pervades the whole church community. This was well exemplified in the work of parishioners raising nearly £100,000 to restore both churches, an effort sustained throughout the last decade of the millennium. These efforts culminated in the restoration of the west window of St Peter's and the installation of floodlighting. And when, in 2000, plaster falling from the roof necessitated further repairs, £40,000 more was raised.

Old St Peter's has a very peaceful atmosphere and its churchyard is full of wild flowers in the spring. Much of the hard physical work of restoration here was carried out by volunteers in the 1990s. The mediæval door of the old church, carbon dated to about 1354, is now back in the church after 600 hours of loving restoration by Elizabeth Viney, a specialist in English period furniture. The bottom of the door was skilfully restored by Rex Palmer of Houghton and the metal frame was made by Just-In Fabrications of London Hill, Stockbridge. The door was then hung by Clearcut, also from London Hill. It was altogether a remarkable achievement by members of the local community.

A valuable part of church and community life is the parish magazine. This serves as a source of news for the town as well as carrying a variety of writing, some religious, some more general. Its monthly production and distribution is the result of hard work by the editor, George McMeekin and a delivery team.

Every church has to raise money and Stockbridge uses many of the usual ways, such as market stalls and bring-and-buys. There are two less common methods. First the three churches, Stockbridge, Longstock and Leckford have teams expert in providing teas, including cream teas. These teams take turns to provide teas in Longstock Park Nursery to visitors to the Longstock Water Gardens on their open days in the spring and summer. They also cater for other occasions, including the church's second money-raising scheme, the Stockbridge Open Gardens weekend. This takes place on a Saturday and Sunday afternoon, usually in August, when ten or twelve gardens are opened to visitors. For a ticket currently costing £2.50, the visitor can wander round a series of gardens of all sizes and types. They can then finish by enjoying a first class cream tea at one of the tables set in front of the church.

Another unusual money-raising enterprise, which supports a number of charities, is Church Mouse Books run by Briar Philips. At the back of the church is a small library of second-hand books for sale. The books are all donated and the sum raised in 2000 reached over £4,000.

Stockbridge Amateur Dramatic Society (S.A.D.S.) by Chris Clark, Chairman

The AmDrams has a long and distinguished history. It was formed in

1933 by a group of local enthusiasts, including Miss Irene Mitchell, Mr Steb Hale and Mr Alick Fowgies. Their first production was a lovely old play called "Ambrose Applejohn's Adventure". The venue was the Town Hall. The stage upstairs is tiny. It is difficult to move scenery, the actors and the audience share the same entrance from downstairs and the audience capacity is limited to one hundred. Despite all the handicaps, however, on a good night, when a play is going well, the atmosphere in the hall can be amazing. It is, in fact, a wonderful little theatre, and, since 1933, S.A.D.S. has regarded the Town Hall as its true and natural home.

Other productions followed in the years leading up to the Second World War. Inevitably there was then an extended interval, but in 1950 the footlights were switched on again with the first of a highly successful series of plays produced by Mrs Olive Brewerton. Olive went on to produce over a score of plays until she retired in the mid-1970s. Since then her advice, wisdom and good humour have been a source of great benefit to a younger generation. Olive liked "a good, well-made play". She set herself high standards. The plays chosen tended to be comedies, farces or thrillers. From a scrapbook of press cuttings of those years it is evident that audiences loved them. Notable performers in this period were Ron Fudge, Margaret Watkinson, Ronnie Pantling, Monica Harding, Becket Pennington-Legh, Mary Butler and Wendy Fenning. Connie Alderman was for many years the much-loved Honorary Secretary of the society.

In the late 1970s S.A.D.S. received an infusion of new talent. New people moving into the area became members, friends were persuaded to join and a team of performers, producers and backstage crew came into being. Since then S.A.D.S. has gone from strength to strength. For several years rip-roaring pantomimes were put on in the Town Hall at Christmas to great popular acclaim.

Other venues have been used: for example, St Mary's Church, Longstock ("Murder in the Cathedral" and "The Boy with a Cart"); Longstock Village Hall ("Private Lives", "Under Milk Wood" and "Toad of Toad Hall") and the garden of Hermit Lodge ("A Voyage Round my Father"). The range of productions has widened considerably: there have been memorable productions of plays by Shakespeare, Chekhov, Ayckbourn, Sheridan, Coward, Wilde, Barrie, Rattigan, Shaffer, Priestley, Fry and other writers. Theatre in the round has been tried ("The Lady's not for Burning"). More recently there have been two, often three, productions a year, with, for the past ten years, an annual open-air play in the beautiful garden of "The Burrow" near Longstock Park. Plays for, and involving, children have featured regularly, with recent performances of "Alice in Wonderland" and "The Wizard of Oz".

So, as its seventieth year approaches, S.A.D.S. is really flourishing. The society comprises a large group of people of all ages and from as far away as Salisbury, who enjoy putting on challenging plays, but in a relaxed, friendly atmosphere. Apart from productions they have an entertaining club evening once a month and the odd bit of socialising. New members are always welcome.

Neighbourhood Watch – Area Co-ordinator Frank Guard

The initiative for creating a Neighbourhood Watch scheme came in 1987 from Mrs Jean Johnson, JP, who approached the local police to arrange a briefing. At a well-attended public meeting it was clear that there was good public support and the police encouraged the scheme. An Area Co-ordinator and 15 local co-ordinators volunteered, each of the latter taking local responsibility, usually for their street or a group of houses. A Longstock scheme followed in 1989 with Area Co-ordinator Geoff Barker taking over this area. Frank Guard has been co-ordinator for the Stockbridge branch throughout.

The aim of Neighbourhood Watch is to deter criminals, mainly by encouraging householders to keep a watchful eye on their neighbours' properties, especially during their absence. It reminds residents of the basic rules of crime prevention: asking for identification from visitors to the house; the regular use of door, window and car locks; keeping valuable garden machinery under lock and key; reporting strange visitors or vehicles to the police; not leaving valuables in a car, even when they are out of sight.

Visitors to the town should know that the commonest type of crime in the locality is break-ins to cars, especially those parked at local beauty spots. Garden sheds and farm building are also targeted for their contents. No-one can say what effect the scheme has but if it only improves contact between neighbours it is worth while.

Medical Services

...climbing a ladder to the cottage bedroom of a man with a perforated peptic ulcer.

After World War Two the town's general practitioner was Dr 'Pix' Loveless[39], who had come to the town, after serving in the First World War, to join his father, Dr W.K. Loveless. In 1951, three years after the beginning of the National Health Service, he was joined by Dr Michael Johnson whose father and brother were GPs in Romsey. Dr Johnson still lives in Stockbridge and has seen the development of medical services over the past 50 years.

In the 1950s and early 1960s the town had changed relatively little from the pre-war era. Few patients had cars or telephones and therefore home visits were common. Housing conditions were often primitive. Dr Johnson recalls climbing a ladder to the cottage bedroom of a man who turned out to have a perforated peptic ulcer. As the junior partner, Dr Johnson took *all* of the night calls. Although at that time few patients called the doctor out unless they were genuinely ill, he would be out at least once a week. Sometimes a member of the family banged on his door because they had no telephone.

The practice was based in a surgery in Dr Loveless' home, Grosvenor Cottage, now Mulberry House. Entry was by a gate in the wall and Geoff Merritt recalls 'The waiting room seated about 8 – 10 people with standing room for another two or three. The rest had to wait outside in all weathers. There were no appointments. It was first come, first served, but everyone was attended to. The adjoining consulting room had paper thin walls and one could almost hear what was going on!' Stan Holdaway remembers the paraffin smell from the stove which provided the only warmth in the waiting room. He also recalls Dr Loveless' kindness. When Stan had chicken pox 'Pix' promised him a bar of chocolate if he didn't scratch the spots. Chocolate was precious in wartime and the bribe worked for all but a very few spots.

In the 1950s there were about 4,000 patients on the list and they were seen by the two doctors, with help from a secretary and with four district nurses, one each in Stockbridge, Chilbolton, King's Somborne and the Wallops. These nurses were very experienced and performed some home deliveries, only calling for a doctor if there were any difficulties. There

[39] He was the third generation of his family to practise in Stockbridge. See the Appendix for the directory entries of 1855, 1895 and 1923.

were outlying surgeries twice a week in the Wallops, King's Somborne and Chilbolton. The main hospital for referrals was the Royal Hampshire County Hospital in Winchester and the consultants there provided excellent support throughout.

In 1961 Dr Loveless retired and Dr Chris Bennett joined the practice. The surgery was moved to Dr Johnson's home, Seven Gables, and two part-time receptionists were employed as well as a secretary. Increasingly patients came by appointment. By the late 1970s a health centre was being promised by health authorities and in the early 1980s land had been purchased in New Street, then still little better than a dirt road. At this stage Dr Johnson retired and Dr Gareth Evans replaced him but the practice continued to use Dr Johnson's house as a surgery because there were delays in funding the proposed health centre.

Eventually, in 1984, money was found and the developments in New Street included a Health Centre: Drs Evans and Bennett moved into the premises in the following year. Soon after, the two-man Broughton practice closed and amalgamated with Stockbridge. The present configuration of health services was established.

Stockbridge Football Club

...there were George, Jack and Ernie Diaper in the 1920s...Jock, Sam and Bess Savage after the War... other family names were Dance, North, Mawson, Webb, Harfield, Miles, Stares, Ridout, Andrews, Langton and Dow.

The only institutions in Stockbridge with a longer history than the football club are the Courts Baron and Leet and the churches. The club was founded in 1894 and has been one of the most successful sides in Hampshire. In 1925 it won the Faber Cup and since then the 'Robins', so-called because of their red shirts, have usually been among the main contenders for honours in local leagues. The early matches were played on Stockbridge Down, but in about 1910 Sir Norman Hill, later the Lord of the Manor, allowed the club to use the field known as 'Little Dean'. It lay to the north of the railway station between the railway line and the A 3057 as it ran from the bottom of London Hill towards Andover, *(fig 25)*. This pitch, with its elevated south-east corner, which is still visible as the small triangular field south-east of the roundabout, was the home of the club for 50 years. Then, in 1970, the road changes which followed the closure of the railway meant that the ground had to be used for the new roads.

An anxious time followed, during which the club used a field lent by Mr John Foord. Miss Elizabeth Viney, a member of the Hampshire Playing Fields Association, was active in seeking funding and a new site. Professor Rosalind Hill offered £2,000 which she had received from the county for the land used for road works. The Vine Inn raised a further £2,000 and there were grants from the Hampshire Playing Fields Association and the Parish Councils of Stockbridge and Longstock.

In 1976 the Stockbridge Recreation Ground Trust, a registered charity, was formed. The site to the north of the telephone exchange was purchased and then began the work of turning a peat meadow into a proper playing field. After many loads of infill material and topsoil and after young volunteers had picked stones out of the soil, a good pitch resulted. Meanwhile fencing was erected and a children's play area was created. The club was back in business. There remained the problem of keeping the recreation ground in good order, which was and is costly. One source of support has been the willingness of the 'Ex-Saints', a team of retired professionals, to play regular exhibition matches against Stockbridge. Over the last 20 years the money raised has amounted to some £20,000. The members of the club, players and supporters, have pulled their weight, cutting the grass and undertaking general maintenance. Despite yearly grants from the Parish Council, the pitch would not be kept in first class condition without the efforts of the football club, so the club and the town both gain.

Between the wars the Stockbridge side was well known as a highly effective team. Although there are no complete records, they won a number of cups. The war interrupted but in the 1950s they had further successes. The loss of the pitch was a major blow and morale and membership sagged, but once the new ground came into use, the team became increasingly successful. In 1979, the first year on the new ground, they became Andover League champions and in 1984 the club was promoted to the Hampshire League, Division 3. That year they also had major cup successes, winning the four major trophies in the area, the only club ever to achieve this. Since then the Robins have progressed to the top flight of the county league, the Hampshire Premier Division.

As the population of the village has altered, only about half of the players have come from the town. However, a core of Stockbridge activists have provided enthusiasm and continuity, some of them the sons and grandsons of people who had played for the club[40]. Dave Webb, for example, once a player and son of Jack Webb, was manager for 20 years and is still active in the club. He provided the information for this section. The family tradition is maintained by the existence of a Veterans side which keeps old hands in touch. Even more important is the provision of a coaching scheme for boys and girls between 6 and 14 years of age. This has echoes of the contribution of Mr Ashberry, Headmaster of the Primary School from 1910. Having played as an amateur for Aston Villa, he was an outstanding football coach for many years, bringing success to both the school side and the town side.

The club's recent successes have brought their own problems. The elevation to the Hants Premier Division has led to a demand by the Football Association that the club install floodlighting and that they build a stand. The necessary planning permission has been given, albeit with some restrictive conditions, but the money has yet to be raised.

The Town Hall – by George McMeekin, Chairman

Stockbridge Town Hall was built in 1790 at the expense of Joseph Foster Barham and George Porter who were seeking election as the two members of parliament for Stockbridge. The construction of the hall was, therefore, something of an election bribe and it seems to have done the trick as both Barham and Porter were returned. The clock tower and clock were added in 1794 and the invoice for this work is in the Stockbridge collection in the Hampshire Record Office in Winchester. Although documentation on the Hall is disappointingly scant, it is thought that originally there was an open market at the front and that the refurbishment carried out in 1810 enclosed this area (which explains the plaque with this date on the front elevation and the date on the clock). This ensured that market traders were protected from the elements. The clock was electrified in 1935. The Town Hall is a Grade 2* listed building.

Over the years the hall has been a centre of many of the town's activities. It served as a temporary church while the present St Peter's was being

---

[40] The family tradition was very strong for much of the 20th century. To quote Bert Earney 'Three Diaper brothers played in the same side in the late 1920s -George, Jack and Ernie – and the Savages – Jock, Sam and Bess – did the same in the post war years.' Other names he quotes are Dance, North, Mawson, Webb, Harfield, Miles, Stares, Ridout, Andrews, Langton and Dow.

built. It also hosted a variety of schools (private, church and board) until the present primary school was built in 1910. At one stage, during the nineteenth century, the hall was owned by the Rector. During the Second World War the hall was taken over by the Army and used for a number of purposes, including a NAAFI store, headquarters of the local Home Guard and for dances. Geoff Merritt recalls that for a time 'during the 40s and early 50s the Town Hall had 'the Pictures' every Monday evening, with two 'houses'. It was 7d to go in and 1d for a cushion. The main film was always the top film of the time such as the 'Desert Rats' with a full programme including a cartoon, a serial, a 'B' film and sometimes the Pathé News.'

At the beginning of the last century, the Town Hall was owned by the Hurford family of Little Dean (originally the Rectory) and was given to the people of Stockbridge by Mary Letitia Hurford as shown on the brass plate above the fireplace in the hall. The hall was then run by elected trustees until 1980 when a new trust scheme, authorised by the Charity Commissioners, came into force. This provided for the ownership of the hall to be vested in the Parish Council, as custodian trustees. Management of the Town Hall remained in the hands of the newly constituted board of trustees, the Management Committee. This includes representatives of many of the organisations that use the hall and is responsible for the upkeep, maintenance and booking arrangements of this important community building.

The Town Hall continues to be used for a wide variety of village activities. The Stockbridge Football Club Social Club has its base on the ground floor and meets regularly. The Mothers and Toddlers Group meets every week, as does the Country Market. The local Citizens' Advice Bureau conducts a weekly surgery in one of the rooms. Stockbridge Amateur Dramatic Society mounts one or two productions a year, with appropriate rehearsal time.

Many groups and organisations hold their meetings in the Hall, including the Parish Council, the manorial Courts Baron and Leet and the Women's section of the Royal British Legion. It is often used as a polling station. In order to provide the additional revenue necessary to maintain the Hall, it is let out when not required for village activities so that antique and craft sales and sales of paintings and plants are frequent occurrences, confirming the importance of the Hall's prime site in the High Street.

The Town Hall, having given valuable service over many years, needs substantial refurbishment. The decor is tired and some of the structure is unwelcoming and inefficient. An ambitious programme has been devised to improve the look of the Hall and the way it works. The stage would be repositioned, the kitchens enlarged and modernised, lavatories improved and expanded and improved disabled access, including the installation of a lift, are planned. The scheme is costly and unfortunately has not attracted Lottery funding. Whatever happens, the remit of the Management Committee remains to improve the Town Hall so that it can continue to provide the amenity to Stockbridge which it has given for over two hundred years.

Chamber of Trade

This was founded in the 1970s when traders got together in response to a threat by Hampshire County Council to restrict parking along the High Street. Their purpose was to represent the interests of businesses in Stockbridge and this is still their objective. They work closely with the Parish Council to achieve their aims. Currently, for example, they are hoping to install CCTV cameras which would cover the High street. There are 32 members and the president is Mrs Mary Tuff and chairman Mrs Marion Paviour.

Scouts, Guides, Cubs, Brownies and Beavers

Scouting in Stockbridge started in 1911, two years after the movement began. The old Scout Hut is behind the Grosvenor Hotel on land given by Professor Rosalind Hill when she was Lady of the Manor. She asked only for an annual rent of one red rose and one shilling and this is presented, to this day, at the annual meeting of the Courts Baron and Leet. The hut came second hand from Upavon, for a total cost of £153.27p. It was brought by Mr Turton on his lorry and Andover 'Toc H' helped with the erection and fitting out.

Over the years many local Scouts achieved their 'Chief Scout's Award', the highest award in scouting. In the 1950s Scouts used to give all the older people in the village six fresh eggs and a bunch of daffodils for Easter. Today there are no longer any Scouts but there is a Cub pack (ages 8-10½) and there has been a Beaver pack (ages 6-8) for almost 10 years. Similarly there are no Guides but there is still a 'Stockbridge' Brownie Guide pack (ages 7-10) though they meet in Chilbolton because most of the pack come from other villages.

8 The Canal and The Railway

Many people know that Stockbridge used to have a railway but fewer realise that before that it had a canal. The idea had been discussed for nearly a century before it opened because Andover businessmen thought that direct access to Southampton would be an advantage. Work finally began in 1789 and it was fully opened in 1795, running from Andover to the tideway at Redbridge. It had 24 locks and a number of public wharves, including one at Stockbridge. In its time it carried a variety of goods including the Normandy stone from Caen used in building St Mary's Church in Andover. It made no profit for its shareholders and eventually closed in 1859.

At that time railways were developing rapidly. After various delays the London and South-Western Railways formed a company, the Andover and Redbridge Railway, to build a new line. They bought the canal and followed

36 The Railway Station in about 1910. The camera is directed southward with the substantial station building on the right. The engine has just come under the road bridge and is arriving at the 'up' platform. The footbridge to the 'down' platform can just be seen. To the left are the railings on the road ramps up to the bridge *(courtesy of Edward Roberts)*

37 Chipperfield elephants outside Wiltshire's bakery, no doubt enjoying some buns. There are keepers on each side and Mr Wiltshire is standing between the two. Elephants on their way to or from their winter quarters were a regular sight in the town until the closure of the railway *(courtesy of Mrs Marjorie Butler)*

its course over 14½ miles, using chalk quarried at various sites[41] to fill it. Another 7¾ miles followed new alignments between the canal sections. The railway ran from Andover Junction Station, the site of the present Andover Station, to Southampton via Romsey. It took six years to complete, opening in March 1865. By that time the company had been taken over by the Midland and South-Western Railway and the initials 'SW' and the connection with the sea at Southampton, led to its nickname, the 'Sprat and Winkle line'. Stockbridge was one of the largest stations on the route.

Initially the line was single track with passing loops at stations. The sharp curves produced by following the canal route led to a number of derailments. As a result, in 1885 the line was realigned in places and the track doubled. By 1892 Southampton was connected directly with Cheltenham via Swindon and Marlborough. A second extension, built in the 1880s, ran north from Fullerton past the Harewood Forest, via Longparish, to join the London – Exeter line just below Whitchurch. This connection enabled Queen Victoria to reach the Isle of Wight from London without passing through tunnels, which she disliked.

[41] One such site is the area now occupied by Medlar Cottage and Tickletrout Cottage in the Houghton Road. A small section of the canal still exists as part of the river system between Timsbury and Romsey.

While the Stockbridge Races continued, racegoers came in large numbers, often on special trains. For many years afterwards horses were transported to the station on their way to and from the local stables. Even after the Second World War it was not unusual to see a string of horses being led along the High Street on their way to Chattis Hill. More remarkably, in the early years of the Second World War, Chipperfield's Circus kept elephants on local farms from time to time. They could be seen in the High Street going to or from the station, *(fig 37)*. This too continued for some years after the War.

Anglers also found the railway convenient. In his book on 'The Trout', published in 1898, the Marquess of Granby remarked that 'The 9.15 A.M. train from Waterloo will take you to Stockbridge or anywhere in those parts, in time to allow you to begin fishing by 12.30, or thereabouts, and to return to London the same evening.'[42]

In both wars the line was heavily used. During the 1914-18 War 6,452 special troop trains and 1,488 ambulance trains passed along the route. In the Second World War the line and its signals were renewed and extended, and bridges were strengthened. Ambulance trains were based at Stockbridge to serve the large military hospital at the top of Winton Hill, behind the present National Trust carpark for Stockbridge Down. Fullerton Junction was doubled in size to serve a large ammunition dump in Harewood Forest.

Between the wars the line was much used by the towns and villages along its length. On Fridays, Andover's market day, traffic there increased as people went to shop. Football specials to and from Southampton were full on Saturdays when Southampton were playing at home. In the period after the Second World War diesel units replaced steam engines. At that stage there was an hourly service from Andover to Portsmouth via Romsey and Eastleigh. This meant that passengers had to change at Romsey for a connection to Southampton. For a time in the 1960s the direct service to Southampton was reinstated but by then use of the line was diminishing. In 1964 passenger services were discontinued. Freight traffic continued until the final closure in 1967. In 1969 the track was lifted.

While the line ran through Andover, it had a level crossing over the

[42] He had been contrasting this with the journeys made by the early members of the Leckford Fishing Club who came down from Northumberland (Chapter 9). He goes on to say 'Undoubtedly in 1800 there did not exist the same conditions of hurry and 'rush' which now seem to pervade the country.'

A303 which at that time went through the town. In the 1950s and early 1960s this caused severe traffic delays and queues back to Bullington Cross, a distance of almost 7 miles, were common on Saturday mornings in summer. The closure of the line relieved this problem and the traffic through the town disappeared altogether when the A303 bypassed Andover in 1965.

The most striking effects of the closure in Stockbridge were the disappearance of the steeply humped road bridge over the line and the demolition of the station. Above and below the town, the line of the railway became the Test Way. The large roundabout at the east end of the High Street then replaced the bridge. A new section of road, which follows the line of the railway through the station, links this roundabout with the second one where the A30 comes down the hill *(fig 27)*. The only evidence that either a canal or a railway ever existed here are the houses in Trafalgar Way called Railway Cottage and Canal Cottage and, behind the telephone exchange, The Wharf. All these changes have brought relative peace to the London Road, once severely burdened with traffic. But some regret the loss of the railway and all it meant to Stockbridge. A romance has been lost.

Sources

Personal communications from Derek Tempero

Mitchell, Vic and Smith, Keith (1990) *Andover to Southampton* Middleton Press. ISBN 0 906520 82 7

Postscript

The playing fields of the Stockbridge Primary School and a woodland area to their north are on the site of the railway sidings. When they were working in a wildlife area in the woodland, the children found coal and clinker and learned about the history of the site. This led to the idea of turning the playshelter into a replica of the Stockbridge Station of the early 1900s and continuing the theme in the playground with a new PE shed being painted as a signal box. There will be a sleeper and ballast path onto the field and a line with the names of the stations of the Sprat and Winkle line along the field to the wild area. Fund-raising is at full steam but it is unlikely that the project will be finished before we go to print.

9 The River Test

The River Test, although only some thirty miles in length, is generally regarded as one of the finest trout streams in England. This is because of special properties which result from the way it, and the surrounding lands, were formed. The story of the river begins in the geological period just after the Jurassic – the Cretaceous. In that era the land which would become southern England formed the bed of a warm shallow ocean, which teemed with life of all kinds. Among the swarms of minute creatures were some with names like 'foraminifera' and 'coccolith algae'[43]. These all contained calcium carbonate, in other words lime. For millions of years they flourished in the warm seas, sinking to the sea-bed when they died. Over long ages the layer thickened and compacted to become chalk, hundreds of metres thick[44]. Chalk is made up of the shells of these tiny beings and because they were full of minute holes, it is porous except where it is very densely compacted.

Later, as continents shifted, this ocean floor was pushed up and became land, buckled and corrugated into valleys and hills, further shaped by later Ice Ages. Initially our river was a tributary of a long 'Solent River' which began at Frome in Somerset and flowed eastward to Littlehampton. Further shifts of land and inroads by the sea broke up this system, the Isle of Wight separated and the Test finished by emptying into what is now Southampton Water.

The Test today – Facts and Figures

The Test rises at Ashe near Overton. The river flows among, and draws its water from, hills which are full of chalk, a total catchment of 1,260 square kilometres or 486 square miles. Above Stockbridge it has contributions from the Bourne Rivulet, the Dever and the Anton. Below Stockbridge it is joined by the Wallop Brook, the Somborne Stream, the Dun, the Tadburn Lake, the Greenhill Lear and the Blackwater. It becomes

---

[43] Loosely translated, foraminifera means 'full of holes' or 'perforated' while coccolith means 'berry-stone'.
[44] To get some idea how thick the chalk is, look at the chalk cliffs on the east side of the valley between King's Somborne and Timsbury – or for that matter at the cliffs near the Needles on the Isle of Wight, or at Beachy Head. Remember too that this is only the chalk above ground or sea level.

tidal at Redbridge and joins the Itchen at the head of Southampton Water.

The porous chalk in the surrounding hills acts as a massive spongy underground reservoir and aquifer, holding the rainfall and feeding it into springs. In an average year 824 mm (32 inches) of rain falls in the catchment region and, apart from some surface run-off, percolates down over several months[45] to reach the river. As a result the maximum flow is usually in the late spring and early summer and is seldom more than 4 - 5 times the minimum. This compares with some 'spate' rivers where the winter run-off can increase flows several hundred times.

When the old bridge was still present there was regular flooding in Stockbridge *(fig 38)* due to its obstructive effect. For example, in 1960 a rainfall of 584mm (about 23 inches) took place over four months and there was much flooding. Since the bridge was rebuilt, flooding has not recurred, except for local floods from blocked drains. Even in 2000, when 605mm of rain fell from September to December, the High Street was free of floods. However by December 2000 the water table in the valley was virtually at river level and water seeped into cellars and into the ground floors of cottages where the floors had been lowered to increase the room height.

Another result of the chalk 'hold-filter-release' effect is that hose-pipe bans have never so far been imposed. The process also produces water which is very clear, a fact which visitors to our town always notice. It is alkaline and hard and its temperature varies from freezing at the edges in a hard winter to 18°C (65° F) in summer.

The Uses of the River

It might seem that today the main use would be providing sport for anglers and this will be considered later. In fact the river also provides water for a number of other purposes of which the most remarkable is in the manufacture, by De La Rue of Overton, of paper for bank notes. Depending on the time of year, between 40% and 70% of the flow at that level is used in making the paper. Virtually all of the water is returned to the river after purification, (Simon Every – personal communication). Water is also withdrawn for domestic supplies, 80% of which is returned to the river after careful treatment[46]. Nowadays more of the water abstracted for

---

[45] When water is drawn from artesian bores it may be well over a year old. (Simon Every – personal communication).

[46] It is only relatively recently that higher standards of purification have applied, as Monica Harding indicates in Chapter 5.

38 Flooding in the High Street in 1915. The Three Cups is recognisable and to its left in the picture is a cottage which was demolished before the present public toilets were built. The boy in the foreground is John Raggio who later wrote the article on the pubs of Stockbridge quoted in the sources for Chapter 3 *(courtesy of Mrs Marjorie Butler)*

domestic use is taken near to the mouth of the river, to minimise the effect on water levels upstream. Other uses are in the ten fish farms on the river system, watercress farms and gravel washing. These activities return almost all the water they use.

In the past the river water found many more uses. It fed the canal and drove mill wheels to grind corn, to process wool, make paper and parchment or tan leather. A Victorian water wheel built to pump spring water up to Longstock Park is still working. But the most striking use, which could still have been seen around Stockbridge until the second World War, was the irrigation of meadows.

Water Meadows

The fields on the valley bottom have seldom been used to grow crops because of the softness of the ground, though some maize is grown for silage. The fields have provided grazing for hundreds of years. In days when labour was cheap and plentiful the meadows were flooded each winter through systems of channels controlled by small sluices[47]. This process dates

[47] The men who engineered and maintained these systems were sometimes called 'drowners'. They could control levels to a fraction of an inch.

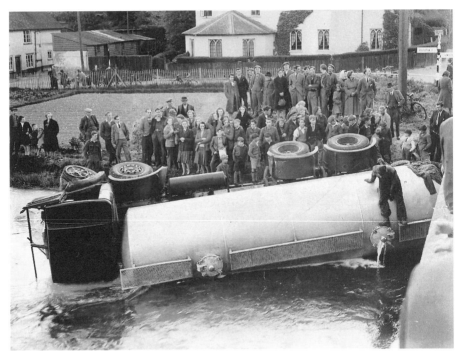

39 A milk tanker in the river in 1947. The driver lost control coming down Salisbury Hill. The photographer is on the bridge looking at the west bank. The crowd are standing in what is now the garden of Lily Cottage. Since then a wall has been built on the road side of this land and tall Leylandii tower over the corner *(courtesy of Ray Standfield)*

back to the sixteenth century. It was widely used in river valleys in England and was only discontinued because it was so labour intensive. Water was spilled over the fields during the winter and kept in place until they were drained in March or later. Incidentally this made an ideal wintering place for duck and snipe.

The agricultural advantages were many. The soil was kept warm; silt and dung from roads and farmyards, together with nitrogen and phosphate leached from arable fields were all deposited on the land, so that the water became cleaner. Some moles were drowned but moles are good swimmers and could often be seen escaping. The result was an earlier and more vigorous growth of grass: many farmers took an early 'bite' for their sheep before flooding the fields a second time. A further benefit was an up to fourfold increase in the crop of hay, but as labour costs increased between the wars it became less common. By the mid-20th century farmers found that artificial fertilisers were easier and cheaper to use and the practice has virtually disappeared. Today the term 'a water meadow' tends to be used for a meadow beside a river but this is not the original meaning.

Man's work has made a 'braided channel system'

The term 'braided' comes from the highly informative fact sheet on the River Test, published by the Environment Agency. It points to the way in which the river has numbers of channels which run this way and that in the valley. Channels have been dug to supply mills, to flood fields, to fill the canal or the earth ponds (so-called 'stews') in which trout were, and still may be, raised. Weirs control river levels and divert water into these streams. At Stockbridge the main river and six other streams pass under the High Street. Often the original use of a channel has long since been abandoned and forgotten, but the many streams of Stockbridge are part of its charm.

Men have also dug peat at various places in the valley. These workings have left shallow ponds at a number of sites, of which the largest, just south of the Common Marsh, is known as the 'Peat Holes'.

FISHING ON THE TEST

Mick Lunn

Mick Lunn, who has given extensive help with this chapter, is one of the best known figures in the world of trout fishing. He was the third generation of his family to serve as Head River Keeper to the Houghton Fishing Club. He was born in Houghton and went to school in Stockbridge and then to the Grammar School in Andover. From the earliest times he was passionately interested in all things to do with fishing and the countryside and often pestered his father for a chance of a day's fishing. He was called up in 1944, was commissioned in the 1st Battalion, the Devonshires, and saw most of his service in the Far East. Even there he found opportunities to fish whenever it was possible. After demobilisation he returned to Stockbridge to start a career with the Houghton Fishing Club. He succeeded his father as head keeper in 1963, retiring in 1992. During his years in the club he took countless distinguished members and guests on the river and many remain his friends today. He has a gift for friendship and is renowned as a raconteur, characteristics which have led him to be in demand as an after dinner speaker.

The Test

The Test provides ideal conditions for fish, especially trout. The water is clean, contains many nutrients and the weeds give an environment where trout can find food and shelter. Soon after the fishing season starts in April, the blizzard of mayfly begins. These flies, which have matured in the river as nymphs, emerge as 'duns' and fly to the nearby trees and bushes. There they shed their coats and develop into the mature form, known as 'spinners'. They are then ready to mate in the air, after which the males are spent: many tumble onto the water and are hungrily seized by trout who welcome the change of diet at the end of the winter. The females fly upstream and lay their eggs, so that the eggs float down as they sink and lodge in the weeds or on the bottom in much the same place as their parents emerged. Many females are also eaten at this stage.

The mayfly are the best known and most spectacular food source, but other flies, such as Olives, Iron Blues, Pale Watery, Sedges and the caddis fly and caenis fly, are hatching through summer and autumn. Other insects which originate on land, such as black gnats and daddy-long-legs, may be blown onto the river and are eaten. Even in winter there is much in the river on which the trout can feed, such as nymphs, shrimps and snails.

The fish are mainly trout, the native brown trout and stocked brown and rainbow trout, with many grayling and some salmon. Pike, bullheads, eels, a few dace and the odd perch are also found. When brown trout and salmon spawn in the river, they need clean gravel on which to do so. This means that river keepers have to see that gravel patches are raked clear of silt. They have many other tasks throughout the year, described by Mick Lunn in his book 'A Particular Lunn'[48]. Their work includes keeping the river banks clear, pollarding overhanging trees, trimming reeds where necessary, maintaining footbridges and hatches, together with the task of cutting the river weeds – in April, June, July and August. Unchecked growth of weeds promotes silting and blockage as well as reducing the clear water available to anglers. Weed cutting is a co-ordinated operation up and down the river, so that the cut weeds do not cause obstruction. Each keeper starts at the downstream end of his section and cuts upstream. During this activity the Environment Agency traps and removes the weed downstream at Timsbury, endeavouring to avoid interference with the salmon fishing in the lower reaches.

Raising Trout

As well as all this work the river keepers have much to do in the hatcheries. Unlike many fish farms the hatcheries run by the Leckford Estate and the Houghton Fishing Club raise trout mainly for stocking rivers and lakes. Raising trout to add to river stocks dates back to the 1890s. Both hatcheries stock their waters with two-thirds brown trout and one-third rainbow. Many of their fish are sold to keepers on other rivers. This, briefly, is how the process works:

In November selected female trout are 'milked' for their eggs, which are then mixed with milt from males. The fertilised eggs are put in tanks fed by spring water drawn from deep bores. The discovery that spring water gave much better results than river water was one of the many contributions made by Mick Lunn's father, Alf Lunn. This water is always clear and its

[48] Mick is the third generation of his family to be Head Keeper to the Houghton Fishing Club. His grandfather, William J Lunn, originator of the Lunn's Particular fly, held the post from 1887 to 1931 – 44 years – and his father, Alfred Walter Lunn, followed him till 1962 and Mick took over in 1963, retiring in 1992. This is a unique family contribution but the Club clearly inspires great loyalty: for example Harry Carey, still living in Stockbridge, worked as a river keeper for 41 years.

temperature is a constant 10°C throughout the year. During the incubation period the eggs are treated daily with a fungicide[49]. After 35 days for rainbow and 42 days for brown trout, the eggs hatch. For a month they live off their yolk sac and then come to the surface. The young fish are called alevin (pronounced 'aler-vin'). They live in the tanks till March or April. Then they are moved to get their first experience of river water in a series of tanks or stews in which they live for the next two years until ready for selling or for stocking the local streams or fishing lakes. Fed daily on specially prepared compounds, they reach a good size much more rapidly than native wild trout, which may take between 5 and 7 years to reach 1½ pounds.

The process is carefully supervised, with regular cleaning of stews or concrete tanks using slaked lime. The result is that trout raised in this way can be exported as disease-free all over Europe, while the reverse is not the case.

Eels

Another 'crop' from the river is its eels. Eels take between 5 and 7 years to mature and at that stage the Test eels are silver in colour. They are caught during their migration towards the river mouth as they set out to travel to mate in the Sargasso Sea. These migrations take place on moonless nights between June and November. In the past the traps were the wire baskets, shaped like flattened cones, which can still be seen just above the road bridge on the Bunny at Longstock. They were lowered into the water facing upstream and the eels were caught in them.

Now these are merely reminders of the past. Today a simpler technique is in use. In certain weirs some of the hatches have horizontal metal grills on the downstream side. These grills are below the upstream water level and above the downstream level so that the water from upstream pours onto them. At eel trapping time the other hatches are closed, forcing all the water through the gridded hatches. Eels can then be picked off the grills and put into tanks of aerated water for transport to market, mainly in London but also in Holland where silver eels from the Test are a great delicacy.

---

[49] At the time of writing this is not strictly true. Malachite green has been used for many years but has recently been banned from use. A decision is awaited on the safety and effectiveness of a newer agent.

40 Mick Lunn fishing on the Test below the King's Mead Weir

The Houghton Fishing Club *by Mick Lunn*

This club, founded in 1822, was, and will always be, a fellowship of anglers dedicated to the pursuit of trout with the fly. Its members set as much store by good companionship as by the fishing itself.

In 1822 in a chance meeting with Mr King, the landlord of the Grosvenor Arms, Canon Beadon[50] discovered that the fishing in the parish of Houghton was to let. Beadon told his friend, Edward Barnard, of this discovery; they looked at the water and took a lease on it. They offered membership at a £10 annual subscription[51] to their friends and named it the Houghton Fishing Club. Needless to say the subscription now is somewhat higher than £10.

The technique of fishing at that time was very different from the methods used today. Fish were caught by 'blowing', using a blow rod (a long bamboo pole) with a line of light floss silk and a natural insect impaled on the hook, for example, a mayfly, grasshopper or large sedge fly. Many of the trees around the river were cut down to let the wind in. This was so that, when the rod was held high, the wind carried the floss line way out over the

[50] Canon Beadon was still fishing at the age of 90 and died aged 101 in 1879.
[51] About £440 at today's values.

stream, mayfly and all, to drop onto the water for the fish to eat. The last recorded time that a fish was caught in this way was in 1904. The 'whipping' rod of the sort we know and use today came in during the late 1800s. This meant that an artificial fly could actually be cast over the rising fish. What a great step forward that was and, by the way, it meant that trees were replanted to keep the wind out!

Through those early years the club gathered together more water. The original lease ran out at Houghton but a year or two later they purchased the water. Lords of the Manor who owned some of the river were often impoverished and were willing to sell. Eventually the members had put together an appreciable fishery which began at the lower end of the Longstock and Leckford water in the north[52] and extended to Houghton and Horsebridge in the south[53]. This is some five to six miles of the valley but with the multiplicity of streams it affords between 14 and 15 miles of fishing.

The Houghton Fishing Club is one of the oldest dry fly fishing clubs in the world, if not the oldest, with fishing diaries which have been kept since 1822. These records tell of every fish caught since that time, recording the name of the rod, where he was fishing, what fly he was using, how many fish he caught, the size of the fish and totals for each year; quite a unique record.

At present there are 24 members and their guests, who fish the water. This is considered to be an ideal number in that the club water gets fished properly. In other words, it does not get over-fished and spoiled, which tends to happen where beats are let out for fishing continuously throughout the week.

About 1800 fish per year are stocked into the club water, in a proportion of 2/3 brown trout to 1/3 rainbow trout. This amount, with the current native wild brown trout, gives anglers what we feel is a good and varied season's sport.

Every fishing club needs a Club Room. For our club it is the curved room over the portico of the Grosvenor Hotel, which the club owns. Here members meet and dine, relax and discuss everything to do with their fishing day. It is truly a fellowship of anglers.

---

[52] The border runs almost straight across the valley from Bottom Road. The Leckford and Longstock water extends northward on the Test to the Mayfly pub and nearly to the Mill at Fullerton on the Anton.
[53] The ownership of fishing rights can be, and in many cases is, different from the ownership of the land. Thus the owners of many properties which border the river are not able to fish in it.

Fishing has been enjoyed at Stockbridge by anglers from all walks of life. During the war many well known servicemen came to fish, such as General Eisenhower and his chief of staff, General Beddell Smith. Mr Lewis Douglas, for a time the American Ambassador to Britain, fished regularly over 20 years. He was a full member for two years and was the only member of the club to hail from another country. Prime Minister Sir Alec Douglas-Home and the Australian Prime Minister, Sir Robert Fraser, were among other distinguished guests. Prince Charles has also fished on the river. For everyone who loves it, fishing is of great therapeutic value. When you are by the river with a rod, the biggest worries in the world disappear.

Other early fishing clubs on the Test

Although the Houghton Club is the only surviving club from the 19th century, two other clubs once existed on the waters of what is now the Leckford Estate. The Leckford Fishing Club began either in 1798 or 1802 and was founded by a group of gentlemen from Northumberland who rented the fishing rights on the Leckford reaches. It appears that they travelled down by stage-coach once a year during the mayfly season. The catches were extremely high in the early 1800s. This club continued until the 1830s when they merged with the Longstock Club.

In 1809 a further club was formed on the west side of the valley, the Longstock Fishing Club. George Tate and Robert Snow were founder members. In 1822 the Reverend Canon Frederick Beadon had accepted a vacancy in the club. Even though, as described earlier, he was a founder of the Houghton Club in the same year, he felt committed to and stayed with the Longstock Club till 1827. At that point the club was in some difficulty as its waters were taken over by a new owner. Some members joined the Houghton Club but by the early 1830s the Longstock Club had found new fishing and was revived. It was joined by the surviving members of the Leckford Club, which moved across the valley probably to get better accommodation and facilities. The club survived, albeit with a change of name to the 'Craven Club', until the early 20th century.

Sources and further reading

Personal communications from David Owen, formerly Managing Director of the Leckford Estate and from Guy Robinson, Head River Keeper to the Leckford Estate.

Bingham, Charles, (1993) *Chalk Stream Salmon and Trout Fishing.* Swan Hill Press

Environment Agency Fact Sheet (1998) *The River Test*

Lunn, Mick and Graham-Ranger, Clive (1991) *A Particular Lunn.* A. C. Black ISBN 07136355223

Poole, Lorna, (1991) *Fishing at Longstock and Leckford.* A paper written for the John Lewis Partnership and held in its archives. Kindly lent by David Owen.

Rackham, Oliver, (1997) *The Illustrated History of the Countryside.* Phoenix Illustrated, London. ISBN 1857999533

10 Greater Stockbridge

Longstock, Leckford and the Leckford Estate

Part of Longstock is closely related to Stockbridge but there are other reasons for discussing Longstock and Leckford in a book about Stockbridge. Their communities have shared many activities. From 1881 to 1932 Longstock Mill (Bradfield's Mill) gave employment to nearly 40 people, including many from Stockbridge. The Anglican churches are linked, sharing a vicar. Activities which are centred on one community are frequently supported by members of the other two; for example, the amateur dramatics. The Stockbridge schools serve all three, as well as other villages and there are many other ways in which they are interrelated though separate. In particular, the Leckford Estate, which owns much of the land in this part of the valley, is of especial interest. So these communities deserve a separate chapter.

Because of the close relationship with the Leckford Estate both villages are to a quite unusual extent, working villages. Many of the people who live in them work locally. Estate-owned houses can be identified by their dark green paintwork, a feature of the John Lewis Partnership. Those living in these houses either work or have worked in the partnership. Leckford is entirely owned by the Estate but the houses in Longstock are of mixed ownership

Longstock

England has many villages which straggle over a considerable distance and Longstock is a good example. It begins in the upper part of the Houghton Road, just across the bridge from Stockbridge proper and ends some 2½ miles (4 km) north, at Longstock Park. Within this spread are two principal concentrations of houses. At the southern end, in what might be called 'Longstock-in-Stockbridge', are houses in the Houghton Road, the lower Longstock Road, Salisbury Hill and Roman Road, together with the Test Valley Secondary School. The other main group is in Longstock proper, extending north from Bottom Road. It is the latter group which might be termed the 'heart' of Longstock with its church, village hall and pub. It is here that the Women's Institute and the Garden Club are based, institutions which do not exist in Stockbridge.

Like all parts of the valley Longstock has features dating from the remote past. Early in the 20th century a copper axe-head or celt (pronounced 'selt') was found in a gravel pit near the river. It came originally from Ireland and has been dated at about 1800 BC. There are large mounds behind Charity Farm which date from the period between 994 and 1042 when the Danes ruled England. These mounds, which have been called the 'Danish Dock', are thought to have been built to house and protect a flotilla of boats. Evidently at that time the river was navigable. Yet from the Iron Age there seems to have been a road running from Salisbury via Quarley and Danebury through Woolbury (the hill-fort above Stockbridge Down) to Winchester and on to Sussex. It crossed the river by a ford at Longstock just below the site of the dock. The ford or 'water-splash' existed until the building of a bridge in 1938.

Local Crafts

It is recorded in the village register of 1865 that there were two blacksmiths, a wheelwright, a bricklayer and two builders, besides a miller, a shoemaker and a maltster. This would have been a normal complement for a village at the time but two other crafts were also based in Longstock. Men from Lancashire came down to cut alder which they took back to make into clogs. Another local industry was the weaving of sedge[55]. Sedge was gathered from the riverside and dried in open sheds for several weeks. Children then had to plait so many yards after school and these plaits were woven and sewn into baskets and mats by adults. This practice was revived in 1919 and flourished for a further 30 years. Even today the local Women's Institute provides weaving and basket-making classes, using sedge among other materials.

---

[55] The sedge family (Cyperaceae) is large and the sub-division of sedges named Carex contain many of the species used in weaving. They differ from grasses in having solid stems, often 3-angled, and flowers all round the stalk instead of in opposing rows.

Longstock and Leckford today

...workers on the farms once registered the passing of time by the times of trains on the railway.

It hardly needs saying that during the 20th century life in these villages underwent many changes. Some are those which have occurred across the nation. Seventy years ago families would be unusual if they went on holiday to Bournemouth. Today a holiday in Spain is quite ordinary. Homes have electricity and modern sanitation. Most households have a car and wives go out to work. While workers on the farms once registered the passing of the hours by the times of trains on the railway, today there is no railway and virtually everyone has a watch. Equally, such deliveries as cattle or fertiliser no longer arrive in the valley by train as they did before the railway closed. Television and the breathalyser have reduced the role of the pub, in this case the Peat Spade, as a social focus. Nowadays the Peat Spade flourishes at least as much as a place to eat at as one at which to drink. Tumbledown cottages have been demolished and new houses have been built. Longstock now has a handsome new village hall. The river in the Bunny has been bridged. Traffic is much heavier, especially on the A3057 in Leckford. Instead of horses, massive tractors move loads. Indeed the fields around are cultivated using machines and techniques undreamt of in earlier times. Even so, a time traveller from 1929 would recognise most of the village without difficulty.

The Longstock Newsletter

A family coming to live in Longstock has a pleasant surprise when a free newsletter drops through their letter-box. Every household receives a copy, published every other month. It carries local news, comments, editorials and articles, together with announcements for forthcoming events. Supported by the Parish Council and produced by the efforts of Chris and Gilly Clark, it is a particularly agreeable feature of Longstock life. Today fewer people meet each other while walking around the village, so local news may not be spread as it once was. Moreover the sheer length of Longstock makes it desirable to have a means of keeping in touch. It was started in 1977 by Geoffrey Snagge and taken over by the Clarks in 1981: long may it continue.

The Women's Institute (WI)

While Stockbridge lacks a WI[56], Longstock and Leckford have had a continuing group since 1918. Today it is still active and valued, with talks on a wide variety of topics. In 2000 the programme has included 'The Leckford Estate', 'Art 'A' Level as a student', 'Early Quakers in Hampshire', 'The Falkland Islands', 'Frosts, Freezes and Fairs', 'Dolls', 'King Arthur – the truth behind the legend' and 'Experiences of a blind man'.

The WI has often seen itself as a chronicler of events. In 1965 it prepared a scrap book of items describing village happenings month by month. This was kindly lent by Mrs Shirley Owen, who was its president in that year. From it we learn that there was an active drama group, a country dancing circle and a youth club offering billiards, boxing, rounders and quizzes. The Leckford Estate had provided land for a playground and the WI had raised the money to equip it. Churchgoers had made kneelers for the church's altar rail. Street lighting had arrived in 1964 and a telephone kiosk had also been achieved. Dustbins were being emptied every other week and the County Library visited on alternate Wednesdays. A bus service had been established. The Test Valley Secondary School, then taking 416 pupils, opened in December 1965. The Cossack Inn, in the Houghton Road, was still serving drinks. It was patronised particularly by stable boys and was regarded as the 'poor man's pub'. Mr Teddy Perry, aged 90, was still digging his own garden!

The scrapbook also notes the state of shooting, which was, as now, a popular pursuit. Bags of 100 pheasants and over 170 duck were being recorded. On the other hand the annual hare shoot in February only yielded some 200 – 250 hares, compared with 500 – 600 in previous years.

Overall the scrapbook gives a picture of a life being enjoyed by the women of Longstock, grateful to be living in the village. It may be that they were conscious that times were changing, since they listed local dialect words still in common use. They were:

> *'lear'* – hungry
> *'shrammed'* – cold
> *'succour'* – a shelter
> *'hanging'* – a steep slope;

[56] The WI in Stockbridge flourished until the late 1960s, ending partly because it lacked leadership and partly because of the deterioration of the Town Hall facilities. Some members joined the Houghton WI and some the Longstock.

'*snell*' – a cold wind;
'*moggy*' – a cow;
'*hunty rump*' – a molehill
'*verlyn*' – a field
'*bunny*' – a large culvert for water

This last is especially interesting, as it may explain the name for the road running east from the Peat Spade across the river bridges.

A scrapbook for the year 2000 is now being assembled. It will no doubt seem as interesting to the next generation as this 1965 scrapbook seems today.

The Village Hall

This is a very fine building. It succeeded an old 1914-18 wooden army hut, much loved in its time, but needing extensive repairs. The new hall opened in 1992. It is very spacious, with room for badminton in the main hall as well as a meeting room, kitchen, stores and a fair sized car park. A particular feature of the lofty main hall is the wall hanging depicting the houses of Longstock in the Test Valley, designed and brought to fruition by Selina Musters. She also created the 'rose' hanging at the other end. Currently she leads a team creating mosaics to go on the ground outside the walls of the hall and she organised the stained glass panels in its front doors.

The hall is the responsibility of the Parish Council but is run by a separate committee. It is available for many different functions and is regularly used by the Badminton Club, the Women's Institute, the Dancing Club, the Garden Club and the Mayflies (a children's group). The charges to such users are not sufficient to pay for all the expenses of upkeep and the committee raises money by a variety of entertainments and by outside lettings.

The Leckford Estate

It was between 1928 and 1932 that John Spedan Lewis bought what is now the Leckford Estate. It later became a part of the John Lewis Partnership. The company has no shareholders and all its profits are returned, in one way or another, to its members, the workforce. This means that about a quarter of the 3,750 acres are used by the partners for amenity and environmental purposes. Five hundred and fifty acres of water-meadows and valley floor woodland surround the fishing beats and lake. There are two nine-hole golf courses and a sports field occupying 150 acres. A further 150 acres are occupied by ornamental gardens including a water garden designed by Spedan Lewis. The remainder of this element of the Estate is given to housing, woodlands and roads.

Spedan Lewis was a man of unusual ability and formidable intellect. Not only a brilliant retailer, he was at one time President of the Classical Society, was a fine chess player and a first class zoologist with a particular interest in lepidoptera, as well as a keen gardener. He implemented the construction of the water gardens which today are opened on twelve Sundays in spring and summer to raise money for charity. He also planted the snowdrops and daffodils which are such a lovely feature of Longstock Park in the spring. All those who knew him speak of his astonishing prescience. 'He looked 30 years ahead and he was usually right'.

The Leckford Estate and the Environment

His interest in natural history made it fitting that the Partnership, on his retirement, set up a John Spedan Lewis Trust for the Advancement of Science which promotes research into environmental and ecological matters. An early count revealed that there are some 1,100 different species of moths and butterflies on the estate. A recent bird census has shown that there are 62 different species breeding, including Montagu's harrier, Cetti's warbler, lapwings and skylarks. This is partly due to its 64 miles of hedge and partly a policy of spring sowing of crops which leaves food for birds, including game birds, in the fields through the winter. Some fields also have 'beetle banks'.

A concern for the environment runs through all the Leckford Estate's activities. For example, in the woodlands around the river, the cycle of growth, death and rebirth of trees is allowed to continue with the minimum of disturbance. This means that wildlife of all kinds are able to flourish. It is, of course, true that some of the estate's practices have been designed to help the rearing of game birds but those who oppose shooting may one day come to acknowledge the uncomfortable fact that providing cover and food for game birds has huge benefits for other birds. In any case there are numerous other ways in which the estate has maintained what is, in effect, a first class nature reserve.

One particular example occurred in the post-war years. There was a proposal emanating from the Ministry of Agriculture to dredge and so deepen the main channel of the Test. This would have emptied the numerous side channels and drained the valley floor, so allowing it to be ploughed and planted. This was fought successfully at the Longstock/Leckford level by the partnership chairman, Sir Bernard Miller. Instead 75 acres were planted with poplars, visible along the Test Way.

How the Estate has Changed

The revolution in agriculture since the War has altered much over the past 50 years. Modern methods and machinery have reduced the numbers needed on the purely farming operations but there have been several developments which have had the effect of increasing its workforce. The first was an example of the way in which Spedan Lewis went his own way against the advice of experts. He wanted to try planting apple trees on the estate and was told that the chalky soil was unsuitable. He persisted and the result is that today there are 230 acres given to fruit, 20% of which is sold in the Leckford Farm Shop, 20% in partnership shops and the rest elsewhere.

Another major change came in the 1980s when legislation was being introduced to ban the burning of straw after harvesting. The then managing director, David Owen, decided to compost the waste straw and this led to the development of a high-tech mushroom farm producing 23 tons of mushrooms each week. This farm alone employs 109 staff.

It would probably be difficult to determine the exact effect of other developments in the estate, such as the trout hatchery or the growth of the Longstock and Leckford Club, but they too have added to employment. Thus, when David Owen joined the Leckford Estate in 1956, it employed 123 workers, with 13 or 14 foremen. Today there are 212 people working on the estate.

The three men who have managed the estate since the Second World War all live in Longstock and have provided much of the material for this chapter.

Maurice Jones read Agriculture at Cambridge before the War. While serving in Singapore he was taken prisoner but survived, returning to this country weighing 8 stones. In 1946 he was appointed as General Manager of the Estate and in the early 1950s took over as Managing Director. He retired in 1980. In his career he had also served as a County Councillor and for two periods, 1985-87 and 1989-91, as Chairman of Hampshire County Council. He was also Chairman of both the primary and secondary schools in Stockbridge. His name can be found on the foundation stone of the Longstock Village Hall.

David Owen came to Longstock in 1956 as General Manager of the Estate and succeeded Maurice Jones as Managing Director in 1980. He too made many contributions to outside bodies. He was Chairman of the National Institute of Agricultural Botany, Chairman of the Test and Itchen Fishing Association as well as a Director of the National Seed Development Association. More locally he was a member and for a time chairman of the Parish Council as well as a Test Valley councillor and Chairman of the Borough's Planning Committee. He retired in 1992.

Malcolm Crabtree took over as Managing Director in 1992. He gained a PhD in Ruminant Nutrition from the University of Aberdeen. He then worked as a consultant for the Agricultural Development and Advisory Service (ADAS), finally becoming Regional Manager of its Midlands and Western Region. He has a major interest in agricultural research and is chairman of the Milk Development Council's R&D Committee. He continues the Estate's connection with NIAB, working on its Herbage Seeds Trial Committee. Like Maurice Jones before him, he is on the Board of Management of Sparsholt College of Agriculture.

[57] The chalk used had to be a highly compressed form, so dense as to be almost a stone or rock. (Kenneth Bramer – personal communication). This contrasts with the pisé form of chalk wall described below in the account of Houghton Lodge. Similar chalk blocks can be seen in Stockbridge. These are the white squares in the wall just behind Lillie. They can be seen to the left across the stream by the path to the Common Marsh.

11 Other Sites Around Stockbridge

Although Stockbridge itself is the focus of this book, there are a number of places of interest in the neighbourhood. These include villages, National Trust areas and hill-forts.

National Trust – The Common Marsh

As explained in Chapter 4, the Common Marsh was once owned by the Lord of the Manor and was given to the National Trust in 1946. Bounded on the east by the Test Way and the west by the Test itself, it occupies 55 acres on the valley floor and the peaty soil gives its turf a springy feel. It is a favourite place for a walk and also provides summer grazing to cattle and horses belonging to local commoners. The bird life once abundant here has diminished, partly reflecting the decline in the country generally but also because many walkers have dogs with them and this discourages ground-nesting birds. However, the river itself has many coot and moorhens, swans and ducks; heron are seen less often. The marsh carries a number of flowers, including marsh thistles, marsh orchids, yellow irises, harebells and, despite repeated efforts to eradicate it, the toxic weed ragwort. The irregular hollows and humps in the middle of the Marsh are the effects of bombs which fell during the Second World War.

Looking north across the Marsh to Stockbridge gives a view across the length of the town, with the spire of St Peter's Church in the centre. Turning to the south, on the high ground to the east, and level with the southern end of the Marsh, is the magnificent white mass of Marsh Court with its many chimneys. In the past Marsh Court has been an important part of Stockbridge life and deserves a separate mention.

Marsh Court

The house was designed in 1902 by Sir Edward Lutyens for Mr Herbert Johnson and the gardens were landscaped by Gertrude Jekyll. It is largely built of chalk blocks[57] which were quarried both nearby and in Brook, on the A3057 south of King's Somborne, where chalk is still quarried. Herbert

41 The unveiling of the War Memorial by Mrs Herbert Johnson in 1921. In the background are the railway bridge and, to the right, the large station building *(courtesy of Mrs Marjorie Butler)*

Johnson was a highly successful stockbroker who loved the area and was a generous benefactor to local causes. He married in 1912 and his wife ran the house as a convalescent home during the First World War. After the war it was through Johnson that Lutyens came to design both the Stockbridge and King's Somborne war memorials, *(fig 41)*. Sadly Mrs Johnson died in 1921. There is a memorial to her in the Winton Hill Cemetery.

Every account of Marsh Court mentions the interesting decorative details, for instance, internally plants and flowers carved in chalk and veneered walnut panelling, while outside the tall chimneys are individual in their design, some spiral, some studded. In 1926 Johnson had become joint master of the Hursley Hunt and Lutyens designed an 80 foot ballroom which blended with the rest of the house. This enabled Johnson to host the Hunt Balls himself! He sold the house in 1932 and its new owner, who was only interested in the shooting, neglected it.

In the Second World War it was briefly home to an evacuated prep school and was later used to house evacuated children and babies. In 1948 it was bought by Maurice Wright and was opened as a boys' preparatory school which later became co-educational. It ran happily and successfully and was very much a part of the local community until 1989 when difficulties forced the Headmaster, then Mr Broadbent, to sell it. It was bought by Mr Geoffrey Robinson who carried out much restoration work on the garden and the house, but sold the estate in 1999. The present owners, Mr and Mrs Stephen Noar, are continuing the restorations particularly in the grounds. In the future they expect to open the garden several times a year.

Stockbridge Down

This is the second part of the National Trust land in Stockbridge. It extends over 160 acres from the B3049 Winchester Road up to Woolbury Ring, the site of an Iron Age fort. Once grazed by sheep under the eye of a shepherd and used for gallops by the racehorses training in stables on Winton Hill, it was invaded by scrub when myxomatosis killed the rabbit population. The Trust have cleared some of the bushes and have had the trees lining the road laid to create a hedge. Within the hedge a fence has been erected to contain the sheep now being used to control the grass. To help this effort, five Highland cattle were introduced in March 2000.

The Down is popular with walkers, especially those with dogs. There is regular riding along the old gallops. Most of those who use the Down are probably unaware that in the eleventh century the knoll in sight of the highway, more or less opposite the car-park, was a site for the execution of criminals. In 1935 and 1936 Dr Gray Hill, while excavating on the Down, found between 45 and 50 buried male bodies. One had concealed under his arm a linen roll containing silver pennies struck in Winchester in 1065. This was called the 'Stockbridge Hoard' and is in the British Museum. Another corpse had beside it a large dog which had been decapitated. There was evidence of a post-hole and it seems highly probable that this was the place where criminals were hanged and left on view in a prominent place, before they were buried.

Some 14 Bronze Age burial sites are scattered at a number of sites on the Down. A curious feature hidden under grass just outside the Down is a 'horse' built out of flints. It lies in private land on the side of the Iron Age hillfort, Woolbury Ring, which lies at the top of the Down. The reason for its presence is uncertain. It has been dated to the 18th century. One unconfirmed story is that it is a memorial to a horse shot by a highwayman, while Professor Rosalind Hill states that it was to commemorate the death of a traveller, attacked and killed at 'Robber's Roost', now the lower car park for the Down. However that may be, mention of Woolbury prompts an account of the early sites in the neighbourhood.

Prehistoric and Roman Sites

The area around Stockbridge has at least four Iron Age settlements, one of which became the site of a Roman villa. There are also many barrows and tumuli, grave-mounds from the prehistoric period. A few of these are shown on Ordnance Survey maps, particularly in the area around Danebury. All such sites, once excavated, are re-covered to protect them, but a visit to Danebury gives a good idea of the sheer scale of the Iron Age defences. This is enhanced by a visit to the Andover Museum and Iron Age Museum which contains some of the finds of the excavations and gives details of the hill-fort construction.

Danebury Hill (143m)

The mass of Danebury Hill *(fig 2)* lies to the north-west of Stockbridge and is a short distance off the road linking the A30 on Salisbury Hill with the A343. Today it has many trees, though diseased beeches on the ramparts have recently been removed. In the time of its main occupation, from about 550 BC to about 100 BC, it would almost certainly have been bare of trees, since they would have obscured the view.

There are no longer wooden stockades around the ramparts which are not as high as they were two thousand years ago. The ditches surrounding the ramparts have partially silted up. The once elaborate gate defences have gone. Yet the site is still a deeply impressive monument to the energy and sophistication of the Iron Age people who lived in this hill-town for four and a half centuries. At a simpler level it provides an enjoyable walk with good views over the surrounding countryside. The overgrown remains of the grandstand of the Danebury racecourse can be seen in the field to the south-east of the hill.

Woolbury (158m)

This hill-fort lies against the northern corner of Stockbridge Down. The centre of the fort is now a field in private ownership and there is little to be seen except for the steep banks around its margins. It was built in the period 600 – 400 BC but was abandoned long before Danebury, somewhere about 350 BC.

Meon Hill

Since some time in the Middle Ages the road to the west of Stockbridge was curved to the north to give a gentler slope to the top of the hill, but the straight line of the original road is still present as a track. On the high ground to the south of this track is the site of an Iron Age farm, excavated in the 1930s.

Houghton Down Iron Age Settlement and Roman Villa

The road from Stockbridge to Danebury runs through land owned by Burnfield Farms. About half a mile from the dual carriageway and to the west of the road is a high point which was the site of Iron Age habitation during two periods (800 – 300 BC and 100 BC – 100 AD) and was then the site of a Roman villa over the period 100 – 400 AD. Professor Barry Cunliffe, who excavated Danebury in the 1970s and 1980s, was in charge of excavations here in 1994. The interest of the findings to archaeologists lay in the details of Iron Age life, in the reasons for the gap in occupation in the middle Iron Age period and also in the reasons for the siting of a large Roman villa on the site of an existing Iron Age settlement.

OTHER VILLAGES

Houghton

Like Longstock, Houghton is a long village, straggling attractively along the line of the Test down to its lowermost element, now called Bossington. It has had many associations with Stockbridge, not least in giving its name to the fishing club. Its population is about 300 and it now has no shops, though there is a garage carrying out servicing and repairs and a pub, the Boot Inn. It is well situated for walks with a number of footpaths, including the Clarendon way, a track along the route of the Roman Road from Winchester to Salisbury. The church, which has a beautiful tiled roof, was begun in the 12th century and has a 15th century wooden tower. The steeple was a Victorian addition and causes problems because its shingles are subject to woodpecker attack! The interior has a number of interesting features, including a 12th or 13th century font.

At the north end of the main village is Houghton Lodge. This property opens its gardens from March to September except on Wednesdays and is well worth a visit for its four main elements. There is a demonstration of hydroponics – the growth of plants in chemical solutions without soil. Then comes a walled garden where the walls are made of compacted chalk[58]. After this the main gardens provide a delightful and varied area extending from the house down to the river. The beautiful and quite unusual 18th century house is an example of a 'cottage orné' and has formed the setting for a number of films and television series.

Further north again is the Dairy Barn, selling farm produce including meat from rare breeds, some of which graze on the fields by the river.

King's Somborne

It is perhaps a little impertinent to write about King's Somborne merely as one of the neighbouring villages, since its population is more than twice that of Stockbridge and it has produced its own book – 'Celebrating Somborne'. It was the centre of the manor to which Stockbridge was attached at the time of the Norman Conquest, but over the years the links have gradually weakened. It remains the mother village for the nearby communities of Up Somborne, Little Somborne, Ashley and Horsebridge. Marsh Court, mentioned earlier, is in the parish of King's Somborne.

It has a primary school, two shops, one with a Post Office, two pubs and two other businesses, one selling all kinds of timber for fencing, agricultural and contracting work, the other hiring contractors' equipment. A filling station and garage recently closed and the site is under development. There are a church, a Methodist chapel and a meeting room for members of the Brethren. The war memorial, like that of Stockbridge, was designed by Lutyens.

Although there are no special sites to visit, the village contains many relics of its important past, as well as a number of examples of the chalk walls which have been discussed above. To the south-west is the area of

[58] This process was once common in the area and corresponds to the 'cob' walls of rammed earth seen in the West Country. A course of flints, or later bricks, was laid to form a base extending above ground level. Chalk was softened by exposure to frost in the winter, and then mixed with straw and moistened to make it workable. This material was then forked onto the wall where it was trampled by men in steel shod boots. Courses were built up a week at a time and then the wall was trimmed and thatched or tiled. This method gave way to the pisé method in which wooden shuttering about a metre high was placed on each side and chalk was compacted with wooden rammers. Once this layer was finished the shuttering was set at the next level and the process repeated. This way was quicker, stronger and did not need straw. These walls need a 'roof' of tile or thatch and a protective surfacing. Where the surfacing has worn away the aggregated chalk looks rather like concrete.

'John O'Gaunt's Deer Park'. This was once an area enclosed by high earth banks and a fence, in which deer were kept for hunting. Within the village there is the Old Palace Farmhouse, which contains residues of the royal palace from the time of Edward the Confessor. He was the king whose association with the village led to its name.

There are two major estates in the parish. Marsh Court has already been mentioned. To the south is the Compton Estate, 3,000 acres containing fine shooting and fishing. It was, until his death in 1989, the home of Sir Thomas Sopwith, the aircraft designer and manufacturer.

Further reading

Cunliffe, Barry (1993). *Danebury* Batsford, London. ISBN 0 7134 6886 6

Marchant, Paul, ed. (1989) *Celebrating Somborne* Somborne and District Society, King's Somborne. ISBN 0 9515 110 09

Somborne and District Society (1992) *Illustrating Somborne* ISBN 0 9595110 2 5

Daniels, Janet; Dougall, Alistair and Livermore, David (2000) *The History of Houghton and Bossington*. BAS Printers Ltd, Over Wallop.

12 Stockbridge and the Millennium

The first meetings to discuss millennial celebrations were held in 1998 and the planning committee, under the chairmanship of David Baseley, was active for nearly two years. Some ideas had to be abandoned because of their cost but hard-working fund-raisers and successful grant applications have brought others to fruition. The list below is compiled in order of the completion of the project.

St Peter's Church

Funds were raised for floodlighting the church and for the restoration of the west window.

Tree planting

The money for this was raised by individual and corporate sponsorship. Under the able and energetic direction of Tony Cathcart-Jones a variety of trees, 50 in all, has been planted, by students from Sparsholt College, at sites around the town. Small brass plates record the names of the donors. The sites are:

A3057 towards Andover, the eastern verge above the northern roundabout

Trafalgar Way verge alongside the White Hart car park

Common Marsh – a pound area in the north-east corner

Common Marsh – along the boundary fence on the eastern side

Stockbridge Down – along the north side of B3049, in the south-west corner

Stockbridge Down – by the car park on the south side of B3049

Passion Play

April 2000 was one of the wettest on record, with many days of continuous rain. In the late afternoon of April 21st, 2000, Good Friday, the weather was showery. But at about 5.00 pm the sun returned and when, at 5.30 the police finally closed the High Street, the first scene, that of Palm

Sunday, began. Fortunately the evening remained sunny apart from a light shower at the time of the crucifixion scene which gave rise to a rainbow over Old St Peter's Church, heightening the intensity of the scene.

The Passion Play was the culmination of over six months of hard work. The production was a joint effort by the churches and the Stockbridge Amateur Dramatic Society, working to a script written by Eve Fulleylove, Frank Saunders and Chris Clark. The Passion Play Committee, led by Chris Clark, found that the biggest problem to overcome was obtaining permission to close

42 A scene from the Passion Play in April 2000. Christ, played by Mike Wilson, is carrying the cross along the path of Old St Peter's Church, escorted by centurions.

the High Street to traffic for the period of the play. However, skilful campaigning by the committee, with support from the media, finally produced enough pressure on the authorities and they agreed to a closure from 5.30 to 7.30. During these negotiations, rehearsals were under way. A total of 30 took place, some in the cold and the wet.

The action of the play was spread along the High Street, beginning in the field just to the west of the Test Bridge and ending in the churchyard of Old St Peter's. Many scenes were played from trailers but the Last Supper took place in St Peter's Church and Pontius Pilate washed his hands of the guilt of Jesus' death from the window of the Houghton Fishing Club room over the portico of the Grosvenor Hotel. As scene followed scene the crowd cramming the High Street moved with the action. Actors not involved in a particular episode moved in among the audience, chatting to those they knew, as presumably could have happened in Jerusalem, even while Jesus

43 The Jubilee Street party of 1935. The tables are in front of The Manse with Sheriff's House on the left. The building on the right is now the Stockbridge Peking *(courtesy of Laurie Stares)*

dragged his cross from the Grosvenor Hotel to Old St Peter's, *(fig 42)*. Once there, the crucifixion and the resurrection were all achieved with simplicity and reverence.

With most costumes made by a team of seamstresses organised by Sue Mansergh; with a large choir and instrumentalists directed by Elizabeth Pakenham; with Stockbridge Riding School providing a mounted escort in Roman costume for Pontius Pilate and a pony for Jesus to lead the Palm Sunday procession; with the Stockbridge Football Club providing 'slaves' to pull the larger trailers, the overall number contributing to the play was about 120. It was truly a great team effort which brought together the people of Stockbridge and many nearby communities and which made a deep impression on the large crowd of spectators. Of particular note was a remarkable performance by a villager, Mike Wilson, in the part of Jesus. His quiet, gentle authority and the agony shown during the trial and crucifixion made a deep impression. Notable, too, were the twelve disciples who, from all parts of the community, came together as a spirited but cohesive group, especially during the splendid and moving re-creation of the Last Supper in St Peter's Church.

44 The Millennial Street Party in Trafalgar Way on June 10, 2000 *(courtesy of John Stephenson)*

Civic Service and Parade

On Sunday May 21st a parade led by Test Valley Brass set off from the Primary School and marched down to St Peter's Church. Many groups in the community were represented, from the Royal British Legion to the Scouts, Guides and Brownies. The new mayor of Test Valley, Mr Tony Hope and his wife, were in a horse-drawn coach while the Lord and Lady of the Manor, Mr Christopher and Mrs Nancy Robathan rode in an open landau. At St Peter's Church an interdenominational service was held, conducted by the Rector, Reverend Peter Aves, and the Baptist minister, Pastor Trevor Timewell. Chris Clark, the Reader, spoke some of the prayers and the Lord of the Manor delivered a beautifully crafted, wide-ranging address covering the past, present and future of the town. He drew particular attention to events, such as the Passion Play, which brought the community together. A reception at the Grosvenor Hotel ended this splendid occasion, which echoed the celebrations, in 1994, commemorating 50 years by Professor Rosalind Hill as Lady of the Manor.

Street Parties and other Celebrations

Stockbridge has held street parties for many occasions, *(fig 43)* and it was agreed that one should be held in the millennial year. The day chosen was June 10th and the weather was fine. When the section of Trafalgar Way leading down to the Test Way was closed, the team led by John Stephenson swung into action, setting out tables and chairs. Participants brought along food and drink and the food was pooled and distributed, *(fig 44)*. A piper played a series of haunting tunes and as the lunch ended a series of entertainments began. While a magician amused and delighted children of all ages, others danced the Gay Gordons and sang old favourites. The Lord of the Manor and the Chairman of the Parish Council distributed a total of 59 millennial mugs to children under 14.

Although Roman Road is in Longstock, its residents were invited to the party. Those who came enjoyed it and this led them to hold their own party on August 5th. It was a great success, with a wide age span, from Jade Cooper at 13 months to Bern Standfield aged 92!

In Longstock itself the main celebration was an outsize Church Fete on September 16th, lasting from 11.00 am till 4.00 pm. With quad bikes, laser shooting, bouncy castles, go-karting, pony rides, Norman-Saxon battle re-enactments and carriage driving in addition to the usual sideshows, it was a considerable success, though attendance was less than hoped for because of petrol shortage due to the blockades of oil refineries at the time.

Town Signs

Another of the actions to mark the Millennium was the purchase and erection of a town sign at each end of the High Street. The occasion was taken to modify the Stockbridge crest and the new version is shown on our back cover.

Publications

The last of the millennial celebrations to be completed was the publication of this book.

Postscript

What the citizens of the future think about Stockbridge today

The pressures of the present-day curriculum are such that it was not thought realistic to ask the pupils of the Primary School and the Test Valley School to provide a full scale chapter on their outlooks and interests. However, they have provided answers to two questions about what they would hope to see preserved and what changes they would welcome.

'What we hope will still be there in Stockbridge in 50 years'

Primary School

§ *The School*
§ *The river and the marsh*
§ *The Grosvenor Hotel and the Church*
§ *The Game Larder*
§ *The High Street*
§ *The wildlife*

Test Valley School

§ *The positive town community atmosphere*
§ *Wild life areas: River Test, the Marsh, the ducks*
§ *The High Street*
§ *The Church*
§ *John Robinson*
§ *Lillie*
§ *The Post Office*
§ *The School*

'What we hope will have changed'

Primary School

§ *Improve the recreation ground and stadium*
§ *Glass bridge over river + glass-bottomed cars*
§ *Improve roads around Test Valley School*
§ *Floating cars so no traffic in Stockbridge*
§ *Ferry all along River Test instead of buses*

Test Valley School

§ *Some more houses*

§ *A shopping centre*

§ *Some take-away shops*

§ *More parking spaces*

§ *More leisure opportunities for younger people, e.g. leisure centre, skateboard park, games.*

The Author's View

Further items which I hope will still be here:

§ *The general look of the High Street*

§ *Stockbridge Down in the care of the National Trust*

§ *The Leckford Estate, still run by the John Lewis Partnership*

My wish-list of changes would add:

§ *Removal of the pylons on the western skyline, with burying of the power lines*

§ *A roundabout at the western end of the town, to slow traffic and allow it to turn round and return to the east*

§ *Absence of litter on the pavements and road verges*

§ *A wider system of safe tracks, allowing walking, cycling and riding away from the road traffic*

§ *A countryside in which children could play alone in safety*

Appendix

SECTION 1 – HISTORICAL

The Origins of the Local Names

When you find names like Stockbridge and Longstock given to neighbouring communities, it is natural to assume that they are connected, but if the experts[59] are to be believed, this is not so.

Longstock. The Old English word 'stoc' could mean a farm and thence 'stoce' or 'stoche', a manor, giving rise to countless villages and towns which end in 'stock', 'stoke' or even 'stow'. One early mention of Longstock is as 'Stoce' in a Charter of King Aethelred, dated AD 982, granting land at Longstock to Leofric. By the Norman Conquest the name 'Stock' was well established. The 'long' was added some time in the next four centuries, presumably because it straggles over such a distance.

Stockbridge. Stockbridge does not appear in the Domesday Book, when the community was part of the 'Hundred[60]' of King's Somborne. At that time it was called either 'White Somborne' or 'Le Strete'. The name 'Stockbridge' does not appear until the 13th Century. The Old English 'stocc' could mean a tree stump or log (whence 'stock still'). The experts think that the name comes from the presence of a log bridge, the Old English 'brugge' or 'brigge' meaning a gangway or bridge. Dr Sandy Burnfield, however, suggests that the bridge was the bridge to 'Stoce', since Longstock does occupy the west bank of the Test.

Leckford. The Old English word for a side-channel or irrigation channel was 'leaht', and became 'leat' in Middle English. A related Danish word is 'lecht'. It is therefore suggested that 'Leatford' or 'Lechtford' became Leckford. Dr Burnfield suggests 'Leofric's ford'.

The River Test. There is little doubt that the name was originally 'Terstan', a Celtic or Anglo-Saxon name but the meaning is uncertain.

Houghton. The Old English name was 'Hohtuninga', the suffix 'ton',

---

[59] 'The Oxford Dictionary of Place Names', 4th Edition, 1980 by Eliot Ekvall, OUP, Oxford, New York and 'The Place Names of Hampshire', 1993 by Richard Coates, Ensign, Southampton.

[60] A hundred was a subdivision of a county with its own court. Originally it was supposed to have a hundred households.

from 'tuninga', meaning a farm or enclosure. It means 'the farm by the spur'. Incidentally, in keeping with its derivation, the local pronunciation is still 'Hoe-ton', not 'Howton'.

The Courts Baron and Leet

A shortened version of the address given on March 15 2000
by Christopher Robathan, MA, Lord of the Manor

Both courts originated from the King who gave the right to hold them to Lords of the Manor. There was no other local government. Winchester and other large towns would play host to visiting justices but travel was difficult and slow. There were county courts and hundred courts but it was left to manors and their parishes to do their own thing. At this lowest level justice was done in what were called either Courts Baron or Courts Leet.

These courts were very different. The more important was the Leet. It met only twice a year, at Easter and at Michaelmas. Its job was to inquire into and decide all matters of local importance – crimes or matters of local administration: it would then either record what was said and see the decisions carried out, or pass serious offenders on to the next tier of justice if the Leet could not punish wrong doers. It was a form of DIY government under the control of the Lord and his steward, with the bailiff seeing their wishes were carried out.

The Court Leet was summoned by the Steward. He could force any person between the ages of 12 and 60 to attend as jurors. There had to be at least 12 in a jury. Only parsons and earls were excluded and if persons did not attend, or having attended refused to take part, they could be fined: this is why we heard our Steward refer to fines earlier this evening. The Steward swore in the officers – the Bailiff, Constable (now called the Sergeant at Mace) and the Hayward. Having sworn in the jury he would harangue it, reminding members what they could do and warning them on pain of hellfire what could happen if they dishonestly failed in their duty.

So what could the Court Leet do? First, it made enquiries at 'ground floor' level of all felonies – for example treason, arson, theft and falsifying coinage. But it could not punish save for the less important crimes: otherwise it would record its findings and pass them on to a superior court for punishment.

Secondly it was concerned with breaches of Common Law (as opposed to Statute Law). It would deal with common nuisances such as complaints of causing a smell, failing to maintain a ditch or allowing a wall or a bridge to fall into disrepair. The court could recommend fines of up to 40 shillings. Equally it sat to decide treasure trove in much the same way as our coroner's courts do now. They also dealt with assaults, trespass, riot and unlawful assembly. They dealt with drunkards, people keeping bawdy houses, those who removed parish boundaries or people described as idlers. Their weapons of punishment were fines, whipping or a time in the stocks. They could punish constables who failed to maintain the stocks, the ducking stool, the pillory or who interfered with the 'pound'.

Thirdly, and I think most interesting of all, the court was the forerunner of today's local government, with the task of considering and making by-laws. They could decide what one particular part of the parish or manor could be used for and when businesses could be opened and closed. As an example today, our Jury will come up and advise me on the date when the Common Marsh is to be opened for cattle and horses and what the charges are to be. Then the jury could punish those who put too much water in the ale, not enough goodness in the bread, those who sold goods under weight or charged too much for them. The jury could punish persons selling bad meat; what was bad and what was good was left to the common sense of the jurors. It is interesting that salmon and trout could not be taken out of the river except in season and then only if salmon were more than fifteen inches and trout more than twelve. One was not allowed to build a cottage on one's own freehold unless there were four acres around it.

The court carried on its discussions in English but its proceedings had to be translated into Latin. Proceedings started at 10 am : the steward then charged the jury with the day's business and proceedings were adjourned until 2 pm when the jury would reassemble and tell the steward their decisions or whether they needed more time.

The Court Baron was a less important court, meeting within the Manor every three weeks when sitting as a freeholder's court or, whenever wanted, as a copyholder's court (copyholders were similar to today's leaseholders). It consisted of the Lord, his tenants, the Steward and the Bailiff, meeting mainly to discuss matters of common concern rather than to administer justice. Personal records were kept – who married whom, when people died, details of tenancies and licences and agreements within the Manor.

For copyholders the length and type of ownership was recorded. Payments could be a rent, a service such as the maintenance of a road or a bridge, the tilling of a field, or provide meat. A tenant might even have to join the Lord's military service in times of disturbance.

When trying matters of dispute the jury was only of three people and its fine was limited to 40 shillings – altogether it had much less authority than the Court Leet.

Rotten boroughs – Gay's verse and Bucket's tombstone

In 1716 it was proposed that there should be a Septennial Act, restricting general elections to one in every seven years. This, of course, threatened the 'takings' of burgesses in Stockbridge and similar boroughs. It drew from the poet John Gay the sardonic verses:

> *'Sad melancholy every visage wears,*
> *What! No election come in seven long years…*
> *…Our streets no more with tides of ale shall float,*
> *Nor cobblers feast six years upon a vote.'*

John Bucket, landlord of the King's Head and negotiator of the payment of £70 each to the electors of Stockbridge in 1790 is buried in the churchyard of Old St Peter's. His tombstone of 1802 carries the flowery epitaph:

> *And is, alas! poor Bucket gone?*
> *Farewell convivial, honest John.*
> *Oft at the well by fateful stroke*
> *Buckets, like pitchers, must be broke.*
> *In this same motley shifting scene*
> *How various have thy fortunes been.*
> *Now lifted high, now sinking low,*
> *Today thy brim would overflow,*
> *Thy bounty then would all supply*
> *To fill and drink and leave thee dry.*
> *Tomorrow sunk as in a well*
> *Content unseen with truth to dwell;*
> *But high, or low, or wet or dry*
> *No rotten stave could malice spy.*
> *Then rise, immortal Bucket, rise*
> *And claim thy station in the skies*
> *'Twixt Amphora and Pisces shine*
> *Still guarding Stockbridge with thy sign.'*

Stockbridge in the County Directories

From the late 18th century until the Second World War there were directories which, county by county, listed towns and villages, with their location, some of their history and characteristics and with the names of the principal citizens. These give a picture of the social composition of communities and are also a useful source of detail about the life of the town. The earliest available for Hampshire, that of 1784, covers the trades and occupations only. Later they give the names of what are variously termed 'gentry' and later 'private residents'. In some the clergy, lawyers and doctors are given in both sections! A number of years have been selected to give a picture of what was happening in Stockbridge as the years passed. In the 20th century it is interesting to see how between the wars, the telephone came into use as shown by the entries with 'TN' for the telephone number. Since the last Kelly's directory was published in 1939, there is no comparable source of information in the post-war years.

Most of the occupations listed in the early entries are still in use but others may not be familiar. At first doctors are listed as 'surgeon and man-midwife'. A 'fell-monger' prepared skins for the tanner; a 'peruke-maker' made wigs; a 'mantua-maker' was a dressmaker (a mantua was a woman's loose outer garment); a 'tallow-chandler' dealt in tallow candles; a 'victualler' might mean someone who sold provisions but generally was an innkeeper, what today would be called a 'licensed victualler'; a 'maltster' made malt used in brewing; an 'excise-officer' collected duty payable on items such as alcoholic drinks and tobacco. A 'huckster' seems originally to have meant a dealer in 'smallwares' – tape, braid, buttons, hooks. The meaning of a hawker or pedlar is probably a later use. Note too the spelling of 'taylor' for 'tailor' in the earlier directories. All of the directories use lower case for the roads, i.e. 'street' not 'Street'. The punctuation has been modified for clarity, with commas after surnames.

1784

George Rich, Bailiff
John Abbot, Constable
Abbot, John, *the Red Lion*
Atkin, John, Grocer
Atwood, John, Cooper
Atwood, Richard, Grocer, Draper and Stationer
Beaumont and Peters, Stone-masons and Common Brewers
Bendall, Mary, Milliner
Binstead, Hugh, Carpenter
Brown, Alexander, Shoemaker
Butterly, William, Blacksmith
Cole, John, Glover and Breeches Maker
Cole, John, Fell-maker
Cole, Thomas, Schoolmaster
Cooper, Thomas, Baker
Corfe, James, Surgeon and Man-midwife
Cully, Joseph, Shoemaker
Dyson, John, Carpenter and Wheeler
Edmunds, John, Grocer and Tea-dealer
Eels, William, Grocer
Everett, John, Wheeler
Fleet, John, Peruke-maker
Fleet, Ann, Midwife
Foster, Richard, *the Ship*
Gill, William, Grocer
Goddard, Matthew, *the Three Cups*
Goddard, John, Bricklayer
Goddard, Sarah, Mantua-maker
Harris, James, *the Swan Inn*, (Post Chaise)
Hayter, Ann, Grocer
Horner, Thomas, Tallow-chandler
Hulbert, John, Breeches-maker
Hulbert, George, Blacksmith
Huskin, Samuel, Carpenter
Leech, Charles, *the New Inn*
Major, Thomas, Surgeon and Man-midwife
Mountain, Mary, *the Angel*
Newman, William, *the King's Head Inn*, Post-Master, &c, (Post Chaise)
Perrin, William, Shoemaker
Phillips, John, *the Plough*
Pickering, Thomas, Butcher
Rawlins, Hugh, Blacksmith
Rogers, Benjamin, Grocer

Sprigg and Beaumont, Haberdashers and Drapers
Terrant, Robert, Bricklayer
Tongs, Robert, Taylor (sic)
Whitten, John, Grocer
Woodyard, Matthias, Carpenter and Joiner
Worley, Ann, Draper and Haberdasher

1796-98

(The exact date is uncertain as it appears to have been issued in stages: it must be after 1795 as the Andover canal is mentioned)
GENTRY
Beaumont, Mrs Mary
Bucket, John, Gent
Hoston, Mr. Thomas
Snook, Mr. Thomas
Windover, Mrs. Susannah
CLERGY
Padden, Rev. Newcombe
Sealey, Rev. Marmaduke
PHYSIC.
Bloxam, ——, Surgeon & Man-midwife
Major, Tho., Surgeon & Man-midwife
TRADERS, &c.
Andrew Andrews, *Bailiff to Charles Wade, Esq.*
Atwood, Henry-William, Cooper and Postmaster
Baldwin, Richard, Carpenter
Beaumont, John, Stonemason
Benstead, Hugh, Carpenter
Bern, Thomas, Peruke-maker
Briant, William, Butcher, &c.
Brown, Harry, Shoemaker
Cole, John, Fellmonger & Breeches-maker
Cole, Stephen, Fellmonger
Cooper, Thomas, Baker
Corff, Richard, Grocer and Linen-draper
Cozier, William, Merchant and Maltster
Cully, Joseph, Shoemaker
Cully, John, Shoemaker
Day, ——, Victualler, (*White Hart*)
Dixon, John, Carpenter
Duff, Simon, Shoemaker
Elton, William, Plumber and Glazier
Elton, John, Thatcher
Evans, Thomas, Grocer and Linen-draper

Gill, William, Shopkeeper
Goddard, Richard, Bricklayer
Goddard, John, Bricklayer & Parish-clerk
Goater, Robert, Shopkeeper
Hamer, Thomas, Carrier
Headach, John, Sadler (surname and trade as spelt)
Hordley, Ann, Linen-draper and Hosier
Horner, Thomas, Tallow-chandler
Horner, William, Maltster
Hughes, William , Taylor and Grocer
Hulbert, John, senior, Fellmonger
Hulbert, John, junior, Fellmonger
Hulbert, William, Huckster
Hulbert, Richard, Smith and Farrier
Hulbert, Richard, Schoolmaster
Kimber, ——, Carpenter
Leach, Charles, Cryer
Maton, James, Carpenter
New, John, Victualler, (*Queen's Head*)
Noyes, John, Farmer
Oliver, Edward, Carpenter
Perrin, Margaret, Shoemaker
Pickering, John, Butcher
Poore, John, Grocer and Carpenter
Rawlins, Hugh, Blacksmith
Reeks, George, Carpenter
Rogers, Hester, Shopkeeper
Russell, Charles, *Ship Inn*
Salter, Charles, Sawyer
Saunders, Andrew, Carpenter and Joiner
Saunders, Moses, Carpenter
Spencer, George, Blacksmith
Steel, William, Clerk of the Wharf
Swain, Rachel, Baker
Tarrant, ——, Victualler, (*Coach-and -Horses*)
Tarrant, Robert, Bricklayer
Thomas, Thomas, Taylor
Tong, Robert, Taylor and Farmer
Tong, Thomas, Taylor and Bailiff
Veal, Samuel, Excise-officer
Whatton, John, Carpenter
Wilkins, John, Victualler, (*Three Cups*)
Wilkinson, William, *King's Head Inn*
Woodger, Matthias, Carpenter
Woodley, Stephen, Shoemaker

Notes: 1. John Bucket, formerly the landlord of the King's Head, is given as a 'Gent.' It is possible that he still owned the inn but was no longer the landlord in residence. 2. The King's Head was on the site of the Grosvenor Hotel.

1855

GENTRY

Attwood, Miss, High street
Chandler, Mrs. Elizabeth, White street
Oliver, Mr. Owen, White street
Parrett, Miss Sarah, High street
Rynd, Rev. Henry Nassau, M.A., (perpetual curate), Winchester Hill
Sadler, Mr. Isaac, High Street

TRADERS

Attwood, John, farmer, East end house
Attwood, Thomas, farmer, Pyle's farm
Barratt, William, *White Hart*, White street
Bedman, William, tailor, High street
Bishop, Robert George, tailor, High street
Carter, Charles, shoemaker, High street
Carter, George, shopkeeper, High street
Coakley, William Tyrrell, chemist & druggist, postmaster & distributor of stamps, High street
Cook, Charles, shoemaker, High street
Cook, George, police sergeant, High street
Cotton, John, hairdresser
Cox, Elisha, saddler & harness maker, High street
Craddock, George, *'Ship'* White street
Elton, Edmund, Plumber &c., High street,
Elton, John, junior, builder & carpenter, White street
Elton, John, senior, baker, High street
Footner, Henry Lintott, agent to the Crown life, clerk to board of guardians, solicitor, & superintendent registrar of births, deaths & marriages, High street
Forder, James, master at Union workhouse
Forder, Sarah, (Mrs.), matron at Union workhouse
Gulliver, George, baker and shopkeeper, High street
Harding, John, cooper, High street

Harris, William, beer retailer & maltster, High street

Hodnet, John, shoemaker, High street

Holley, Stephen, fellmonger & parchment manufacturer, High street

Hopkins, Ann (Miss), school, High street

Hopkins, Thomas, horse breaker, High street

Hulbert, Geo. draper & grocer, High street

Hulbert, Geo. Sen. blacksmith, High street

Hulbert, Richard, parish clerk, High street

Hulbert, William New, 'Three Cups' High street

Jolliffe, James, school, High street

King, Young, horse trainer, White street

Larcomb, Samuel, carrier, High street

Lavington, James, 'Vine', & butcher, High street

Loveless, William Ker, surgeon, High street,

Lush, Thomas, coal merchant, High street

Marsh, Henry, carrier, High street

Newman, John, corn dealer & coal merchant, High street

Pearse, Ann (Mrs.), milliner, High street

Nicholson, John, stationer, agent to Hope life, & Medical, Legal & General mutual life assurance companies, watch & clock maker, & toy dealer, High street

Paice, Charles Edward, *Grosvenor Arms posting & commercial hotel,* High street

Rowe, Frederick, shopkeeper, '*Waggon & Horses*, High street

Rowe, George, baker & grocer, High street

Sadler, William Thomas, horse trainer, White street

Scott, Samuel, horse trainer, Houghton Down

Smith, Thomas, china & glass dealer, High street

Spencer, Henry Cole, butcher, grocer & ironmonger, High street

Touge, Henry, beer retailer, High street

Varcoe, John, linen draper, High street

Wetton, William, builder & shopkeeper, High street

Wilkins, Richard, blacksmith, High street

Wilkinson, John, draper, grocer & beer retailer, High street

Worth, Thomas, plumber &c., High street

Notes: 1. The street names are included for interest. 'White street' is the same as London Road today but did include the White Hart. 2. At some point between 1830 and 1847 the Coach & Horses became the Waggon & Horses.

1895

PRIVATE RESIDENTS

Barnes, Robert Newton, Grosvenor cottage

Capel, Christopher, Grosvenor house

Carlisle, Major Anthony, Winchester hill

Chandler, Rev. Richard John, T.A.K.C.L. (rector & chaplain of the union & rural dean of Stockbridge)

Cotton, Rev. William, (Congregational) High street

Crawford, Mrs., Winton hill

Duff, Mrs., High street

Grace, Mrs., The Ferns

Grice, Barcham, High street

Hulbert, John

Hurford, Henry Robert, Brightlands

Lancashire, Hicks Withers, Manor cottage, Winchester Hill

Loveless, Walter King, Steepleton

Oliver, Osmond, Hillside house

Russell, Robert Henry

Squire, William, Springfield house

COMMERCIAL

Atwell, Henry William, *Ship Inn*

Barnes, Robert Newton, surgeon, Grosvenor cottage

Breadmore, Alfred George, maltster & corn merchant High street

Brown, Charles, farmer, Phillip's heath

Brock, Charles, cowkeeper & confectioner, High street

Brown, Ellen (Miss), shopkeeper, High street

Bugden, Thomas, beer retailer, High street

Carter, Samuel, butcher, High street

Colls, Thomas, general draper & house furnisher

Cooper, Frederick William, tailor, High street

Domoney, Elizabeth (Mrs.), beer retailer, High street

Dyas, Charles Edward, *Queen's Head P.H.*

Fry, Cornelius Keel, grocer, baker & draper, High street

Gardener, John, *Three Cups P.H.*, High street

Gauntlett, John, beer retailer, High street

Gilbert, Henry Herbert, builder and parish clerk, High street

Goodfellow, William, *Vine P.H.. High street*

Grosvenor Family & Commercial hotel & posting house (Thomas Cannon, proprietor; Robert Henry Russell, manager), wine & spirit merchant & refreshment contractor, High street

Hale, Frederick, plumber, High street

Hale, Thomas, shoe maker, High street

Harris, James, keeper for the Stockbridge Fishing club, High street

Henwood, Allen, boot maker

Holley, Willie, fellmonger & parchment manufacturer, High street

Hudson, John, sporting correspondent, High street

Hewitt, John, watch maker, High street

Hulbert, George, land surveyor, & post office, High st

Jacob, Emily (Mrs.), saddler, High street

Joyce, George, inspector of permanent way for S.W. Railway Co., High street

Kellow, John, bricklayer

Loveless, Walter King, L.R.C.P. Edin., surgeon, medical officer to the union & medical officer to the workhouse & superintendent registrar, Steepleton

Maynard, Frederick, *White Hart P.H.* & veterinary surgeon

Miles, Harry, sporting correspondent, High street

Mouland, Isaac, farmer, East End house

Neal, George, plumber, High street

North, Josiah, chemist & wine & spirit merchant, High street

North, Louis, horse dealer, High street

Palmer, John, builder

Portsmouth Infantry Brigade (Bearer Co.) (Surgeon Captain Walter King Loveless, commanding)

Roe, John, brewer, High street

Rolfe, George, blacksmith

Selfe, Henry, beer retailer, High street

Smith, George, farmer, Manor farm

Spencer, Henry Cole, butcher, High street

Stockbridge Conservative Working Men's Association (Major Anthony Carlisle, president)

Stockbridge Fishing Club (H.G.H. Norman esq. Hon.. sec.), Grosvenor hotel

Strangeways, Colville, Inland revenue officer, High st.

Teasdale, Thomas, grocer & baker, High street

Tiley, John, chimney sweeper

Vearncombe, Hugh Legge, shoeing smith, cart & waggon builder, machinist & farmer, High street

Ventham, George, newsagent, High street

Ventham, Richard, coal dealer, High street

Volunteer Battalion (1st) Hampshire Regiment (T Co.) (Captain Robert Hewitt J.P. commandant; William Stevens, sergeant instructor)

Wakeford, John, relieving & vaccination officer & collector to the guardians, registrar of births, deaths & marriages, High street

Webster, Ben, sporting correspondent, High street

Webster, Samuel, *Waggon & Horses P.H.*, High street

Worth, Alfred Charles, deputy registrar of marriages

Wilson, John, butcher, High street

Wiltshire, John, farmer, Upper Sandydown

1923

PRIVATE RESIDENTS

Brannon, Charles H., Winton lodge

Bryant, George Rourke, Little Dean house

Chandler, Rev. Richard John, T. A. K.C.L., High street

Hill, Sir Arthur Norman bart, Green Place Winch'ter Hl

Johnstone, Mrs. C.M., The White house

Kelly, Major John Calver, Belle Vue house

Lewis, Daniel A., Springfield house

Loveless, Maynard Lambert, Grosvenor cottage

Loveless, Walter King, Steepleton

Munn, Mrs. M., The Little house

Murly-Gotto, Percy, Atners tower

Stratton, Henry George, Trevena

Swan, Mrs. J.M., Hillside
Vearncombe, Miss, The Nook
COMMERCIAL
Berriman, George, blacksmith, High street
Chant, Job, plumber & painter, High street
Colls, Thomas, ironmonger, High street
Davis, Rose (Miss), parish nurse, London road
Drummer, William, grocer, see Ferguson & Drummer
Dumper, Arthur, boot & shoe repairer, High street
Dunford, George Edward, dairyman, High street
Earney, Bertie Augustine, *Vine Inn*, High street
Every, Alfred Harry, police sergeant, High st, T.N.17
Ferguson & Drummer, grocers, High street
Fowgies, Herbert, builder, deputy registrar of births, deaths & marriages & clerk to Parish Council, High st.
Gibbs, Henry Joseph, motor engineer, High st., T.N. 25
Goater, John, shopkeeper, High street
Goater, Walter, chimney sweeper, High street
Goddard, Goddard, water keeper for the Houghton Fishing Club, High street
Hale & Son, plumbers, High street
Hale, Charles, shoe maker, High street
Harfield, Charles, taxi-cab proprietor, High street
Hewitt, John, watch repairer, High street
Higgins, Francis Alex. cycle agent, High street
Hopkins, John Ed. *Waggon & Horses P.H.*, High street
Houghton Fishing Club, (A.N. Gilbey, hon. sec.), Grosvenor hotel
Institute, (The) (J. Ferguson, hon. sec.)
Jacob, Bethell, saddler, High street
Jerome, Herbert Arthur, butcher, High street
Kent, William David, greengrocer, High street
Lane, Frank, carpenter, High street
Lee, Samuel, wheelwright, High street
Lloyds Bank Ltd. (sub-branch), open tues. & fri. 10 a.m. to 12.30 p.m., High street
Loveless, Maynard Lambert M.R.C.S Eng., L.R.C.P. Lond., physician & surgeon, Grosvenor cottage

Loveless, Walter King, L.R.C.P. & S. Edin., surgeon, medical officer to the union & the poor law institution, med. off health Stockbridge Rural District Council & supt. registrar Stockbridge district, Steepleton. T.N. 4
Lovelock, Joseph, boot repairer, London Road
Mack, Albert & Son, hauliers, Winchester Road
Miles, Henry, sporting correspondent, High street
Miles, Harold John, hair dresser, High street
Ministry of Labour Employment Exchanges, Branch Employment Office, (C. Hale, branch mger.) High st.
Mitchell, Ernest William, relieving & vaccination officer & collector to the guardians & registrar of births, deaths & marriages, assistant overseer & collector of rates, Whiton house
Murly-Gotto, fruit, plant & vegetable grower; also motor haulage between Bath, Bristol, Salisbury, Bournemouth & Southampton; prices on application for haulage by ton or package. Atners Tower farm. Telegraphic address, "Gotto, Stockbridge"
Murray, Martha (Mrs.), laundry, High street
Neale, Branwell Henry George, farmer, Manor farm
Orpwood, William, shopkeeper, High street
Parker, Thomas, cycle agent, High street
Prebble, Albert Ed'd, motor car garage, High st T.N. 11
Sartin, Edward, draper, High street
Selfe, Ellen (Miss), beer retailer, High street
Shelton, Charlie, *Grosvenor hotel*, High street, T.N. 9
Short, Louisa (Mrs.), dress maker, High street
Standfield, William James, assistant overseer &clerk to the Parish Council for Longstock, & agent for Hants General & Friendly Society, Trafalgar house
Staples, William, temperance hotel, London Road
Stares, Sydney, butcher, High street
Stratton, Henry George, grocer, High street
Tabor, Thomas George, grocer
Talbot, Sydney Garson, draper, High street
Taylor, Albert, boot repairer, London road

Thomas, Gater, Bradfield & Co. Limited, millers
Turton, Alfred, coal dealer, High street
Ventham, Richard Burgess, coal dealer
Westminster Bank Ltd. (sub branch) (open wed. 10.30 a.m. to 12.30 p.m.), High street
Whiffen, John, *White Hart hotel*
Wiltshire, Frank, baker, High street, T.N. 19
Winchester Hill Posting Co. Limited, bill posters & advertising contractors

1939

PRIVATE RESIDENTS
Corrall, James W., Mead house
Green, Miss Mary Addison, Old Rectory
Hill, Sir (Arthur) Norman bart, Green Place, Winchester Hill
Jameson, Lt.-Col. J. Bland, C.I.E., Atners Tower
Johnstone, Mrs C.M., The White house
Kewley, Col. Edward Rigby D.S.O., M.C., Little Dean house
Loveless, Maynard Lambert, Grosvenor cottage
Morris, Miss Hilda Grace, Old Rectory
Nicholson, Misses, Shepherd's close
Percival, Helier George, Winton lodge
Smyth, Captain Sydney Keith, R.N. (ret.), Meadow-brook
Starkey, John B., Little house
Vearncombe, Miss, The Limes, Winton hill
Winn, Walter James Gardiner, Manor farm

COMMERCIAL
Barter, Frank, water keeper for the Houghton Fishing Club, High street
Bridge Temperance Hotel, High street (Mrs. J. Bartley, proprietor)
British Legion Club (H.C. Harfield, hon. sec.) High st.
Brown, Charles, hairdresser & tobacconist, High street
Compton, Ada (Mrs.), dressmaker
Corrall & Son, butchers, High street
Cox, William George, baker, High street, T N 88
Cozens, Edith (Mrs.) photographic dlr. High st. T N 83

Cozens, Fredk. Geo., insur. agent, High street T N 83
Critchell, John Henry, farm bailiff to Col. E.R. Kewley, D.S.O., M.C., North Park farm
Dumper & Son, boot & shoe repairers; bed & breakfast; electric light throughout (C.T.C.) High street
Easterbee, Charles, horse trainer, Winchester rd. T N 5
Fielder, T.W. (L. Fielder) Trevena, Winton hill T N 26
Fielder, Thos. (Mrs.), boarding house, Trevena, Winton hill T N 26
Foord, Walter, farmer, Fairview. T N 57
Fowgies, Herbert & Son, builders, High street T N 27
Fowgies, H., clerk to Parish Council, High st. T N 27
Greyhound P.H. (Thos. Spearing) High street T N 104
Grosvenor Garage (Fenning & Son, proprietors.) High street T N 11
Grosvenor Hotel (family & commercial) (Charlie Skelton, manager) High street T N 9
Hale, Charles G.M., shoe maker, draper, tailor & outfitter, High street T N 32
Hale, Harold, smallholder
Harfield, Henry Chas., taxi-cab propr. High st. T N 71
Hewitt, John, watch repairer, High street
Higgins, Fras. Alex., motor car garage, High st. T N 36
Houghton Fishing Club (R. P. Page, hon. sec.), Grosvenor hotel,
Jacob, Arabella Ethel (Mrs.), saddler, High street
Jeanes, Ellen (Mrs.), shopkeeper, High street
Jerome, Herbert Arthur, butcher, High street T N 51
Kent, Caroline Mary (Mrs.), greengrocer & seedsman, High street
Kilby, S.J. Ltd. grocers T N 8
Lane, Frank, ironmonger, High street
Lee, Samuel, builder, High street
Lloyds Bank Ltd. (sub-branch), open tues. & thurs, 10 a.m. to 12.30 p.m. High street

Loveless, Maynard Lambert, B.A., M.R.C.S. Eng., L.R.C.P. Lond. surgeon, medical officer to the Stockbridge district, Stockbridge Area Guardians Committee, Grosvenor cottage T N 4

Lovelock, Joseph, boot repairer, London road

Miles, Alfred Harry, sporting correspondent, High st.

Ministry of Employment Exchanges, Branch Employment Office, (C. Hale, branch manager), High street T N 32

Motley, W.A., poultry farmer, Wynrush. London hill T N 23

Mowatt, Lilian C. (Mrs.), shopkeeper, High street

North, William Stanley, dairyman, High street

Orpwood, William, shopkeeper, High street

Parker, Thomas Farnham, cycle agent, High street T N 118

Pierce, W.J., chemist, High street, T N 64

Seven Gables Guest House (R. G. Waldy, propr) T N 61

Snelgrove, Herbert Hy. Geo., dairyman, High street

Southern Counties Agricultural Trading Society Ltd. (The) , corn & flour merchants, Station yard T N 65

Stares, Sydney Rt. & Son, butchers, High street T N 14

Stockbridge Motors, motor engineers. T N 108

Stockbridge Telephone Exchange, Trafalgar house,

Stratton, Henry George, grocer & provision merchant, High street T N 51

Taylor, Albert, boot repairer, London road

Turton, Alfred, coal & coke dealer & haulier, London road T N 103

Vine Inn (Mrs. Harriett Ellen Hills) High street

Waggon & Horses P.H. (John E. Hopkins) High street

Whiffen, Cyril Gordon, newsagent, High street T N 61

White Hart Hotel (Frederick Pike)

Williamson, A. Yarrow (Miss), nurse, High street

Wiltshire, Frank, baker, High street T N 19

2000

INTERNET WEBSITES

Stockbridge (general website): www.Stockbridge.org.uk

Robjents: www.robjents.co.uk

The Stockbridge Peking: www.stockbridgepeking.co.uk

Courcoux & Courcoux: www.courcoux.co.uk

Wykeham Galleries: www.wykeham-galleries.co.uk

SECTION 2 – THE PRESENT DAY

People, Institutions and Organisations contributing to Stockbridge Life

Chapter 7 discussed some of the organisations which play a part in Stockbridge life. There are many more which cannot be discussed in such detail and there are many individuals who give time and energy to help run the organisations. For the record some of this information is given here.

Member of Parliament for Romsey

In March 2000 the MP, Mr Michael Colvin and his wife, Nichola, died tragically in a fire at their home in Tangley. At the subsequent by-election on May 4, Mrs Sandra Gidley was returned as the new MP.

LOCAL GOVERNMENT
Hampshire County Council, The Castle, Winchester

This has overall responsibility for local government in Hampshire and it supervises such matters as the highways, education and some aspects of the environment. The precise demarcation of responsibilities between county and borough councils is often difficult to define but those involved say that 'it seems to work'. The local councillor is Mr Michael Woodhall.

Test Valley Borough Council, Beech Hurst, Andover, and Duttons Road, Romsey

Many of the local services are provided by the Test Valley council. These include refuse collection, public sector housing, leisure services, parks and street cleaning. They are also responsible for deciding on planning applications. The local councillor is Mr Daniel Busk.

Parish Council

The membership is: *Chairman*, David Baseley; *Vice-Chairman,* Tony Cathcart-Jones; *Clerk*, Kenrick Fell; *Members,* Owen Bates, John Foord, Marjory Gilmour, David Gray, Shirley Guard, Mick Lunn, James Ridley, John Robinson.

The Parish Council meets monthly except in August. The Annual Parish Meeting is in April. The current number of parishioners is about 485.

The Churches

Anglican: the United Benefice of Stockbridge and Longstock and Leckford

    Rector of Stockbridge and Leckford and Vicar of Longstock: Reverend Peter Aves (Rev Aves resigned in October, 2000)

    Honorary Assistant Priest: Canon JFO Bown

    Reader: Mr Christopher Clark

    Editor of the Benefice Magazine: Lt Col G McMeekin

Parish of St Peter, Stockbridge

    Churchwardens: Mrs P Clarke; Maj Gen J Stephenson

    Deputy Wardens: Mrs P Webster; Lt Col G McMeekin

    Honorary Secretary: Mr M Wilson

    Honorary Treasurer: Lt Col G McMeekin

Parish of St Mary, Longstock

    Churchwardens: Mr C Reynell; Mr N Tatton-Brown

    Honorary Secretary: Mrs M Andrews

    Honorary Treasurer: Mrs A Rogers

Parish of St Nicholas' Leckford

    Churchwardens: Mrs B Monaghan; Mr R Watt

    Deputy Warden: Mr L Creed

    Honorary Treasurer: Mr A Monaghan

    Honorary Secretary: Miss S Mansergh

Roman Catholic: St Thomas More Church

The attending priests from St John the Baptist Church, Andover, are led by Father Kieran Flynn, S.M.M.

Baptist: Steadman Memorial Chapel

    Visiting Lay Pastor: Pastor Trevor Timewell

Other groups, organisations and committees in Stockbridge, Longstock and Leckford

This list is taken from the Parish Magazines up to October 2000 but omits some names already mentioned in the text. It provides a picture of many more of the activities in the town. The names of individuals are those who are the 'lead individuals'.

Beavers ~ Sylvia Baker

Bell Ringers (Longstock) ~ Christopher Reynell

Bell Ringers (Stockbridge) ~ David Webster

Benefice Choir ~ Peter Aves

Brownie Guides ~ Jane O'Boyle (Brown Owl)

Church Mouse Books ~ Briar Philips

Cub Scouts ~ Sandy Hammett

Dr Barnardo's ~ Shirley Guard

Evergreens (Stockbridge) ~ Nan Clay

Joy Rides Shopping Bus ~ Gilly Clark

Leckford Cricket Club ~ Nigel Marriott

Longstock Garden Club ~ Peter Rogers

Longstock Neighbourhood Watch ~ Geoff Barker

Longstock Parish Council ~ David Burnfield (Chairman); Elaine Merritt (Clerk)

Longstock Village Hall ~ Marjorie Andrews; Selina Musters

Longstock and Leckford WI ~ Marjorie Andrews

Music With Mummy ~ Jennifer Palmer

Royal British Legion (Stockbridge Women's Section) ~ Joan Hiscock

Royal British Legion (Houghton And District Branch) ~ John Stephenson (President); Michael Ford (Chairman); Peter Penwill (Secretary); George McMeekin (Treasurer)

Royal Air Force Association ~ Ben Warren

Rupert Trust ~ Alasdair Cox

Stockbridge Carnival Committee ~ Dave Watts

Stockbridge Conservative Branch ~ Neville Whiteley; Janet Whiteley

Stockbridge Football Club ~ David Gray

Stockbridge Town Hall ~ George McMeekin (Chairman); Elisabeth Weigall (Secretary); Dave Webb (Bookings); Barry Mitchell (Maintenance)

Stockbridge Baby And Toddler Group ~ Linda Aves

Stockbridge Country Market ~ Marjorie Stares

Test Valley NSPCC ~ Felicity Hellier

Index

The buildings and enterprises in the High Street, listed in Chapter 6, are not included in this index.